A Short Guide to Writing
about History

£9.99

THE SHORT GUIDE SERIES
Under the Editorship of
Sylvan Barnet
Marcia Stubbs

A Short Guide to Writing about History

second edition

RICHARD MARIUS
Harvard University

■ HarperCollinsCollegePublishers

Acquisitions Editor: Patricia Rossi
Project Editor: Thomas R. Farrell
Text Design: Alice Fernandes-Brown
Cover Design: Wendy Fredericks and Kay Petronio
Cover Photo: Comstock Inc.
Electronic Production Manager: Angel Gonzalez Jr.
Desktop Administrator: LaToya Wigfall
Manufacturing Administrator: Alexandra Odulak
Electronic Page Makeup: RR Donnelley Barbados
Printer and Binder: RR Donnelley & Sons Company
Cover Printer: RR Donnelley & Sons Company

A Short Guide to Writing about History, Second Edition

Library of Congress Cataloging-in-Publication Data
Marius, Richard
    A short guide to writing about history / Richard Marius. — 2nd ed.
      p.   cm.
    Includes index.
    ISBN 0-673-52348-9
    1. Historiography.   2. History—Methodology.   3. History—Research.   I.
Title.
    D13.M294   1994   94-8774
907'.2—dc20   CIP

95 96 97 9 8 7 6 5 4

*For my sons Richard,
Fred and John.
For the miles we have
biked together
following history
under the soft skies of France.*

Contents

Preface

This little book arose out of my experience of teaching European history for sixteen years—first at Gettysburg College and then at my alma mater, the University of Tennessee—and then out of the sixteen years I spent directing the Expository Writing Program at Harvard, where I regularly taught a course called "Writing about History."

Most students came into my courses believing that history was hardly more than a collection of names and dates to be memorized and repeated on examinations. If they had written a paper about history in high school, they had usually chosen a broad subject, gone to the library, looked up several articles in encyclopedias, and stitched together a pastiche of secondhand thoughts without ever imagining that they themselves were supposed to think about the data. It was my job to teach them that history becomes most exciting when we study primary sources—the basic stuff from which history is made—to try to make sense of them and to tell a story about them.

To write history is to tell a story about the past. Every time we tell a story, we answer questions: On what authority do we tell the story? Is the story true? What parts of it do we know better than others? What caused the events of the story to happen? Are elements of this story like those in other stories we know? What makes this story unique? What makes it worth telling? The questions are endless. Their variety and complexity make history a fascinating discipline.

The best reasons for studying history are the same as those for studying all the liberal arts: Historical study satisfies curiosity. Only someone with a stump for a head is not curious about how things got to be the way they are. History also provides us with the pleasure of vicarious experience, of living through our study lives that we can never live for ourselves. It opens windows into the variety of human experience and reveals human nature not in some abstract philosophical way but in the concrete actuality of what human beings think and do. History tells us how diverse human beings and their societies can be. If we study it attentively, it should make us more tolerant of people unlike ourselves.

One of the greatest developments in historical study in recent years has been its expansion. Only a generation or two ago, historians thought that the only history worth attention consisted of war and politics and that the only historical figures worth studying were great men. Now we study the history of women, black history, the history of the family, gay and lesbian history, the history of popular culture, the history of science, and heaven knows what else. Everything has a history; when history is written well about any topic, an audience waits to read it.

Teaching history has been for me a means of showing my students that they have worthwhile thoughts and can use them to write interesting and original essays about history. While I was working on this second edition, I taught a class of sixteen first-year students. I gave them a packet of primary sources, which I had photocopied, and turned them loose to write four papers about four different historical topics.

One topic was a 1919 murder trial in Knoxville, Tennessee, when a young black man named Maurice Mays was convicted of a murder he almost certainly did not commit. He died in the electric chair in 1922. The stories about the trial in the afternoon paper, the Knoxville *Sentinel,* were remarkable and appalling for the attitudes they displayed toward black Americans. The judicial opinion in the decision of the Tennessee Supreme Court refusing to overturn a lower court's death sentence was equally intriguing. These stories rather than the trial itself became the subjects of essays my students wrote.

My students also wrote the story of the battles of Lexington and Concord as it came out of British and Patriot sources. They wrote about the early Ku Klux Klan and its apologists. And they wrote about the controversy between fundamentalists and "modernists" early in this century over the proper way to read the Bible. They did what historians do: They took primary sources and tried to make sense of them. They realized that they could think about these sources, come to plausible conclusions, arrive at substantial agreement—but still not agree with each other in important matters. I told them I wanted them to write a story that a roommate could understand without having to seek them out to ask questions. Roommates not in the course suddenly found themselves acting as guinea pigs to see if an essay on something they knew little about was comprehensible. We discovered together the intellectual excitement of writing essays for which we had to read between the lines of documents to discover the premises of the writers. Most of my students were enthusiastic about the course. I hope they learned something not only about writing history but also about approaching any texts they will encounter in life. History makes us ask questions and try to answer them, and it leaves us always with some questions that may remain mysterious; any text should do the same.

The first edition of this little book met with surprising success. Patricia Rossi of HarperCollins asked me to revise it to make it shorter and more usable, and she has been steadfast in her support and patience through these past months. John Wyeth, her editorial assistant at HarperCollins, and I have talked many times by telephone as the revision has gone along, and I appreciate his efficiency, geniality, and patience.

Above all, I am grateful to the hard-working and careful reviewers who made important suggestions that I have tried to incorporate in this edition—Professors Douglas Ambrose of Hamilton College, Charles T. Evans of Northern Virginia Community College, Dee Garrison of Rutgers University, Gayle Gullett of Indiana University Northwest, and Paul T. Mason of Duquesne University.

I must also express gratitude to my students in the Expository Writing Program of Harvard who have used the book through the years and helped me see it better. (I have always donated the royalties earned from my own students to various student publications around the University.) I am also delighted to have correspondence about the book by those who use it out in the country at large.

For more than twenty-five years, my wife, Lanier Smythe, has tramped with me through battlefields, graveyards, churches, temples, museums, towns, and village, guidebooks in hand, while we sought to satisfy our historical curiosity about what we saw. On our many bicycle trips in France, often with sons Richard, Fred, and John, we have never been able to bypass anything that seemed to have the slightest historical interest. She is a college teacher herself, a first-rate art historian, and she has helped me to see much more of what I was looking at than I could ever have seen without her. She has made me understand how much of history cannot be confined to words alone. But her own witty words are a delight; we share through the years the pleasures of past and present.

Many other dear friends sustain me by their enduring affection and loyalty through many years. I mention here especially Ralph and Connie Norman, Milton and Margaret Klein, John and Judy Fox, W. C. Burriss Young, Stephen Williams, Linda Simon, Rod Kessler, Sarah Abrams, Ron and Renata Fleming, Doug and Rene Bryant, Ted and Maud Wilcox, and my brother John. My sons, to whom the book is dedicated, remain friends, too.

RICHARD MARIUS

A Short Guide to Writing about History

Introduction

Students struggling over an essay in history have often told me that they know the subject but cannot write about it. They usually mean that they have a jumble of facts in their heads but cannot tell a story about them.

Their complaint represents a discovery: History is a special kind of thinking. It involves telling a story, and while facts are essential in telling a story, they are not enough. You can have a big, bad wolf; a little girl named Red Riding Hood; an old grandmother; a basket of cakes; and a dark woods without having a story. You can even know the date of the wolf's birth, the color of Red Riding Hood's hair, and the mailing address of the grandmother as well as her Social Security number, and still not have a story.

Stories have tension, usually right at the beginning. At the start we know that something is going to happen. People or forces contend with each other. Readers see tension, struggle, and the possibility that something may go wrong, and they read on to see how it all comes out. In writing an essay about history, you tell the story of your thinking about a topic wherein forces oppose each other with the outcome in doubt.

Historians study sources that tell them about the past, and they write because they see something in these sources that needs to be explained. Like journalists, they ask who, what, where, when, and why. What happened? Who was responsible? Where did this event happen? When or in what order did things happen? Why did they happen? What have other historians said about the event? What mistakes did they make that I can now correct? The historian is a curious and relentless questioner.

Historians are like most of the rest of us: They are curious. They want to know what things mean. When the people of Israel crossed the Jordan River into the Promised Land after their Exodus from Egypt and their wandering in the desert for forty years, their leader

1

Joshua had them set up twelve stones. He said that in years to come when children asked their parents, "What do you mean by these stones?" the parents would tell the story of how Israel crossed the Jordan with God's help. The stones were a memorial; that is, they made Israel remember. They made children ask questions that adults answered.

All historical writing begins as an effort to answer questions. We find a puzzle and try to solve it. When you write a paper for one of your history courses, you must do the same—find a problem that stirs your curiosity and try to solve it. If you don't have a problem, you don't have a paper.

Here are the first two paragraphs of a splendid article in the *American Historical Review*, the leading journal for historians in the United States:

> In France during the 1920s, fashion was a highly charged issue. In 1925, an article in *L'oeuvre* jocularly described how the fashion of short hair had completely overturned life in a small French village. After the first woman in the village cut her hair, accompanied by "tears and grinding of teeth" on the part of her family, the fashion had quickly become "epidemic: from house to house, it took its victims." A gardener swore he would lock up his daughter until her hair grew back; a husband believed that his wife had dishonored him. A scandalized curé decided to preach a sermon about it, but "unfortunately he had chosen the wrong day, since it was the feast of Jeanne d'Arc." As he began to condemn bobbed hair as indecent and unchristian, "the most impudent young ladies of the parish pointed insolently at the statue of the liberator." By claiming the bobbed-cut Joan of Arc as their mascot, these young women grounded their quest for "liberation" in the rich, tangled mainstream of French history. They appealed to the ambivalent yet strongly traditional image of *Jeanne la pucelle* (Joan the Virgin), at once patriotic, fervently Christian, and sexually ambiguous.
>
> The fashion among young women for short, bobbed hair created enormous tensions within the French family. Throughout the decade, newspapers recorded lurid tales, including one husband in the provinces who sequestered his wife for bobbing her hair and another father who reportedly killed his daughter for the same reason. A father in Dijon sought legal action against a hairdresser in 1925 for cutting the hair of his daughter without his authority. "At present, the question of short hair is dividing families," argued Antoine, one of the hairdressers who pioneered the bobbed cut. "The result," according to journalist Paul Reboux, "was that during family meals,

nothing is heard except the clicking of the forks on the porcelain." One working-class woman, who was in her twenties during the era, remembered that her mother-in-law did not talk to her sister-in-law Simone for almost a year after the latter bobbed her hair. René Rambaud, another hairdresser who helped to popularize the cut, recalled the story of a newly married woman who cut her hair, believing that she had the right to do so without consulting her parents. Her mother and father in turn accused her husband and his parents of the monstrous crime, leading to a rift so severe that the two families did not reconcile for twenty years.[1]

We read these anecdotes, and we ask ourselves, "What was all the fuss about?" Professor Mary Louise Roberts will explain the fuss in her lucid and compelling article. By the time we get to the end of her essay, we understand the meaning of the uproar over "bobbed" hair. Here is her last paragraph:

> For historians trying to understand socio-cultural changes during the period of World War I, the controversy surrounding postwar fashion is a rich source for exploration. The ways in which French observers read the text of fashion can tell us much about what preoccupied and worried them during this time of transition. Many of the French, such as fashion's critics, yearned for a more traditional and stable French society, symbolized by the domestic hearth. They expressed anxiety that change would usher in a colder, more impersonal world. Others, namely the supporters of fashion, welcomed change as a dismissal of pre-war social constraints. Fashion was not "politics" as we are used to conceiving of it, but the debates over its meaning in postwar France were profoundly political. The fashions of the modern woman became central to the cultural mythology of the era, instilling at once envy, admiration, frustration, and horror, because they provided both a visual language for upheaval and changed and figured in a political struggle for the redefinition of female identity.[2]

Professor Roberts was stirred by curiosity, and she sought the answer to a question: Why did the French after World War I make so much of the decision of some women to cut their hair short? We look at the issue today and find it utterly puzzling that anyone should care

---

[1]Mary Louise Roberts, "Samson and Delilah Revisited: The Politics of Women's Fashion in 1920s France," *The American Historical Review*, June 1993, pp. 657–658. I have left out Professor Roberts's extensive footnotes for these paragraphs.

[2]Roberts, p. 684.

whether women cut their hair or not. That puzzle is precisely what interests Professor Roberts, and she writes an essay to solve it

All this involves science and art. Science is a synonym for knowledge. But knowledge of what? History includes data—evidence, the names of people and places, when things happened, where they happened, bits of information gathered from many sources. It also includes interpretations of historians and others in the past who have written on any topic that any historian decides to treat in the present. The art of history lies in combining fact and interpretation to tell a story about the past. That is what Professor Roberts does in her article. She has data—the reports of the quarrels and bitterness aroused in France when women started cutting their hair short after World War I. Her essay is an interpretation of what the data mean.

As times passes, legends and lies creep into history. Historians try to distinguish between the true and the false. In the sixteenth century some English writers called history "authentic stories" to distinguish it from fantastic tales about the past. Historians in the Renaissance set about examining sources, making judgments about what could be believed and what was implausible. They searched for old documents, studied them to see if they were authentic, weeded out forgeries, and compared copies to find errors that scribes had made in transmitting texts. They also compared different stories told about the same events. These historians tried to tell the truth—as do historians today.

But in the study of history, "truth" is complicated, contradictory, and usually obscure. History does not repeat itself. Every historical event happens one time and becomes separated from the present by the steady accumulation of other events happening day by day. We cannot put the assassination of President John F. Kennedy into a laboratory and make it happen again and again as we might conduct an experiment in chemistry, measuring and calculating to see precisely the relations between cause and effect. The event happened once—on November 22, 1963—and it will never happen again. To know that event we are dependent on the memories of those who were there and, as they die off, on the records they left us of Kennedy's death. These records may include sound and video recordings that make his murder more vivid than books and articles can do. But they are still records, subject to many interpretations and subject also to the tricks memory plays even on eyewitnesses. We can never relive the event exactly as it happened.

All historians confront an essential problem: The past is dissolving under our feet all the time. The Romans had a proverb: *Tempus edax rerum,* "Time the devourer of things." Time destroys. The evidence for past events is always incomplete and fragmentary, like a jigsaw puzzle washed out of a shipwreck and cast upon a rocky beach by the waves. Many pieces are lost. Those that remain are often faded and warped. Historians fit the pieces together as carefully as possible but holes remain in the picture they are trying to reconstruct. They do their best to fill in the holes with inferences that seem plausible and that fit the available facts. What emerges may closely resemble what happened, but we can never be sure that what we know as history has got it exactly right. Our knowledge of history is always in flux, and historians are always in dialogue not only with the primary sources of events they write about but also with other historians of those events. To write history is to be engaged in an eternal argument.

THE STUDY OF HISTORY AS A WAY OF THINKING

History and writing are inseparable. We cannot know history well unless we write about it. Writing allows us to arrange events and our thoughts, study our work, weed out contradictions, get names and places right, and question interpretations—our own and those of other historians. In writing we work out the chronological order of events—not a simple task but one indispensable to the historian's craft.

Fluent talkers can touch on first one idea and then another, sometimes using body language to stress a point, and overwhelming the opposition by charisma or by mere loudness and discourtesy when their argument is weak. They may depend on someone else in the group to help out when their logic or facts fail.

Writers perform a much more daring act. They must develop an idea with logic and clarity and with the boldness that arises from the confidence that a reader can study their words again and again and discover that the words add up to a plausible statement, given the evidence. Writers cannot hide their thoughts. If their thinking is illogical, unfair, untruthful, confused or foolish, their words are right there on the page to be attacked by anyone with the care and the interest to look. Good talkers can contradict themselves, waffle, and weasel— and on being called to task can claim that their hearers misunderstood them. Because our short-term memories are so fallible, we may think that we have indeed misunderstood. Also, because we are usually polite in groups, we may allow talkers to escape from the trap of their own confused expression by their dexterity in shifting words. Writers enjoy no such emergency exit. What they have said they have said, and it is there for all to see again and again.

Socrates complained to Phaedrus in a dialogue by Plato that "writing is unfortunately like painting; for the creations of the painter have the attitude of life, and yet if you ask them a question they preserve a solemn silence." He meant that writing cannot talk back. Writing is only what is there on the page. If written words "are maltreated or abused," says Socrates, "they have no parent to protect them; and they cannot protect or defend themselves." Socrates believed that speaking was much superior to writing—although we know everything that we know about him from dialogues written down by his disciple Plato. And we also see Socrates dominating all the conversations so that his students do not have the chance to ask questions that we wish we could have asked him. His main point is worth pondering: Writers must be sure to write as clearly as possible so their words can stand alone and be understood.

Clear writing goes hand in hand with a certain sense of human possibility and limitation. No wonder that in some societies, such as that of ancient Israel, historians were priestly figures. They wrote in the light of their beliefs about the relation of God to humankind and therefore with a certain definition of human nature. Today in a secular world, historians explicitly or implicitly deal with human nature. Our beliefs about what is possible for human beings control our beliefs about what might have happened in the past. Can we be heroic? Are we always selfish, or can we be truly generous? Does human history move in response to leaders? Or are leaders thrust up by the society that in fact leads them? Are our strongest motivations economic or sexual? Do we have a natural aggressiveness, or are we naturally peace loving? What motivates decisions?

A student of mine once wrote that in 1215 King John of England "decided" to give the English people Magna Carta and guarantee them certain liberties. He made it sound as if King John had been struck one day with a benevolent impulse and decided on his own to give his people a gift. I remarked that in history, those who have power give it up or allow it to be reduced only when they are forced to do so. The real story of Magna Carta is not, therefore, King John's benevolence but the forces that made him issue the document. In such a light, the story of Magna Carta becomes in part a story of human nature.

As important as any other question about human nature is this: Do we have any freedom of choice? Is history a series of important decisions that could have gone either way? Or is it a masquerade, a perpetual series of predestined events that no human will can control? Did Robert E. Lee have to fight the battle of Gettysburg the way he did, or did he have a choice? Did President Harry Truman have a choice about how he might have responded to the Soviet Union after World War II? Or was he compelled by events to become a cold warrior?

Historians nearly always write as if the people they write about had the power to choose. The tension between what they chose and what they might have done gives history its excitement. Herbert Butterfield, a philosopher of history, wrote, "History deals with the drama of human life as the affair of individual personalities, possessing self-consciousness, intellect, and freedom."[3] Tolstoy, by contrast, in his novel *War and Peace,* wrestled with the idea of freedom, observing that "to conceive a man perfectly free, not subject to the law of necessity, we must conceive a man *outside of space, outside of time, and free from all dependence on cause.*[4] He wrestled with the problem of just how much freedom we have and what part of life is constrained by necessity. He concluded that leaders only *seem* to lead— that in fact they emerge out of the collective working of a power inherent in the masses of people.

In writing about the past, historians may not say explicitly that their answers depend on their view of human nature or human freedom. Yet their answers depend on assumptions, sometimes unexpressed, about what is possible or probable in human nature and what is not.

Our times and our thoughts are largely shaped by the past. That shaping is one reason we study history. How we think, how we react to occasions of daily life, the vocabulary we use in speaking of the past—all are legacies. To study the past may help us understand better how we came to be who we are. These discoveries then help us decide what we want to retain from the past and what we want to reject. By showing us that our lives are historically conditioned, we discover a certain freedom. We know that what *is* does not have to be this way.

[3]Herbert Butterfield, *Christianity and History,* New York, Scribner's, 1950, p. 26.

[4]Leo Tolstoy, *War and Peace,* trans. Constance Garnett, New York, Modern Library, n.d., p. 1131.

Every part of the past has a unique quality. Every event we study in history existed in its own network of cause and effect, its own set of relations between people and events, its own modes of thought, usually taken for granted by the societies themselves, often assumed to be a divine ordination that could not be changed. A thunderstorm roars over the Kansas prairie today, and the television news meteorologist in his bright suit and his hair spray explains it as the result of a collision between a cold front and a warm front. In ancient Mesopotamia, the Babylonians heard the thunder as the voice of their storm god Marduk and thought that he was throwing lightning bolts at the earth. In these and countless other ways, spontaneous responses to many experiences in the past were different from our own. Part of our task is to work our way back into that past mindset so that we think about experience as people in different times thought of it. Yet we can never fully abandon our own perceptions; we cannot recover the past exactly as people at a given time thought of life and the world.

Sometimes historians endeavor to perceive the unique qualities in events and the qualities that seem to repeat themselves. For example, what qualities help some large states endure, and what qualities doom others to fall? The earliest great empires in Western civilization were made possible by the domestication of the horse shortly after 2000 B.C. The horse allowed the swift passage of armies and imperial emissaries from place to place, and armed horsemen struck terror into the ranks of soldiers inexperienced with the noise and speed of such mighty animals. Those empires rose swiftly and swiftly collapsed. But then the Roman Empire rose and endured for centuries. What circumstances made these early empires rise and fall with bewildering speed? How was Rome different? Why did the Roman Empire endure for so long? Would our study of Assyria and Babylon illuminate in any way our understanding the collapse of the Soviet Union? The question is fascinating, but the answers are uncertain. One historian may see a pattern of repetition; another may see in the same events circumstances unique to a specific time and place.

Few historians would now claim that history allows us to predict the future; the old cliché that history repeats itself is not true. Some broad patterns repeat themselves—empires, countries, and cultures rise and fall. Protests against a dominant culture often show up in how people—especially young people—dress and wear their hair. To some, these repetitions make it seem that the entire process of human history is locked into invariable cycles. History becomes a treadmill on which human beings toil endlessly without getting anywhere.

But on close investigation, the swirls and waves of the historical process do not appear to move in predictable patterns. Those who assume that learning about the past will allow them to avoid mistakes in the future underestimate the continuous flow of the new into human events. New inventions or new ways of thinking or new combinations can upset all predictions. In 1914 both the French and the German generals in charge of planning for a war between their two countries expected the coming conflict to resemble the war between Germany and France in 1870–1871. In that earlier war, the Germans moved swiftly by railroad and on horseback, outmaneuvered the French, and determined the outcome of the war within three months. Although Paris did not fall to the Germans until 1871, the French were beaten in the field by September 1870 in a war that began in July. It was a war of motion—dramatic, soon over, without much damage either in destroyed property or in human life.

The generals on both sides in 1914 expected a short war, not realizing the power of a new weapon, the machine gun, which slaughtered advancing soldiers in unimaginable numbers, creating a daily massacre that turned the conflict into a four-year standoff in opposing lines of trenches running from the Swiss border across France to the English Channel. In this long, hard war, millions died, and the north of France was devastated.

In 1940 the French, learning from the fatal experience of World War I, built a series of concrete forts across northern France called the Maginot Line, anticipating another war in which armies would face each other until one dropped from exhaustion. The French planned without considering the new technology of that era—the airplanes and the swift armored tanks used by the Germans to defeat the French army in forty days of *blitzkrieg*—lightning war—during the summer.

At the very least, experiences such as these teach us to be cautious in suggesting what history can predict. Our own contemporary experience confirms this caution. In recent decades, thousands of historians young and old have studied the history of the Soviet Union. The Central Intelligence Agency employed thousands more scholars and spies over the years to help our government predict what might happen to the Soviet Union in the future. Yet not one of these people predicted anything like the sudden collapse and breakup of this great empire in 1989 and 1990.

And what about the place of leaders in history? The current mood in historical studies is to be skeptical about how much individual leaders may accomplish on their own; we seem to be closer to Tolstoy than to Butterfield. Historians know that any particular event in history is brought into being by a huge network of contributing forces—some clearly visible and some difficult to identify. What caused the American Revolution? The traditional answer has been oppression of American colonies by Britain, the mother country, and most of us can probably recite a number of events in that oppression that we learned in grade school—the Stamp Act, the Boston Massacre, the Boston Tea Party, and finally the skirmishes at Lexington and Concord on April 19, 1775, when someone fired "the shot heard 'round the world." Individual leaders such as John Hancock, Sam Adams, John Adams, James Otis, and others in Massachusetts appeared for many years to have been leaders of an almost unanimous populace, rallied by their oratory and their example to resist the oppressor. That, at least, was the history of the American Revolution as many of us learned it in grade school and in popular mythology spread by Fourth of July oratory.

On examination, British "oppression" seems much less severe than was once commonly supposed, American support for the Revolution far less than unanimous, and the leadership of the patriot forces much more ambiguous. Historians now search for deeper causes that provoked a substantial number of Americans to want their independence from Great Britain enough to fight for it. Orators are nothing unless they have an audience, and our experience in the present may show us that orators do not so much convince people to change their minds as they provide words for feelings that people already have. What groups were dissatisfied and willing to listen to the patriot orators? Why? What groups were content under British rule and why? What role did American women and the American clergy play? To what degree was the American Revolution a class struggle within colonial American society? How much of the Revolution's success came because the British were more concerned with their war with France? Here is a puzzle where there are many more pieces than "leaders" and "followers." Here are two complex populations, Americans and British, in continual flux with not only different motivations but different degrees of intensity and different resources. Somehow out of this confused mix, the American Revolution happened.

Historians nowadays do not reject the role of the individual altogether. Biography remains the form of history most read by the general American public, and biographies by their nature emphasize the individual. Still, a mood among historians sees the individual working under more complicated restraints, with more ambiguity and with both less success and less abject failure than biographers once admitted. We have moved away from the Renaissance view of history that held it to be a collection of moral examples. From the Renaissance until modern times, biographers attempted to provide heroes to be imitated or villains whose examples were to be avoided. Now the emphasis is much less judgmental, and the motive of biographers is to tell a balanced story and to explain rather than to condemn or praise.

Historians now study sources and deal with issues that once drew little attention at all. For centuries the writing of history was almost entirely about what men did. If women entered the story, it was because they did things male historians generally expected men to do: They ruled countries as did Queen Elizabeth I of England; they refined radium, as Marie Curie did in France; they wrote novels, as many women have done for several centuries. Historians usually neglected women in all fields, but they were willing to give some limited attention to women who, in the view of the historian, acted like men. Now historians are turning to many other areas of historical interest—the role of women in the home, the woman laborer in factories and on farms, styles of motherhood, women in settlement houses, women as immigrants, the voting patterns of women, the influence of fashion in determining women's role in society, and so on. Black history, immigrant history, labor history, sexual history, the history of fashion, the history of sports—all are modern interests of historians working away at uncovering as much of the human experience as possible and leading the profession of history itself away from the notion that to understand the past we need only understand the personalities and the decisions of a few important male leaders.

Whatever its subject, the study of history is an unending detective story. Historians try to solve mysteries in the evidence and to tell a story that will give order to the confusion of facts that we can know about the past. Historians make connections, assign causes, trace effects, make comparisons, uncover patterns, locate dead ends, and find those influences that continue through the generations until the present.

We encounter history by reading and writing. We read books and articles, and slowly we gain some understanding of the shape of the past, the general framework within which events took place. When we study history in college, we write about the past using the methods of professional historians. Writing helps us think about what we know, and of course it helps our teachers see what we know and how we are thinking.

This little book will guide you through the major steps in writing papers in history for college undergraduate classes. Inevitably, such a book must discuss some of the issues historians face in historical study when they write. It must also deal with some issues in writing that writers confront in all disciplines. This is a book both about methods in historical study and about methods in writing. It should give you some understanding of general problems underlying all historical study, and it should help your writing in all courses that you take in the college or university. It should make you a better detective, and a better teller of some of the innumerable stories that taken together make up the study of the past.

1

The Essay in History

We saw in the introduction that history is far more than an assembly of facts; it is the writer's interpretation of facts that raise questions, provoke curiosity, and make us ask the questions who, what, where, when, and why.

This chapter will provide a checklist to help you study your own historical work to see if it conforms to the expectations readers of history bring to books and articles. We bring to everything we read the expectations we have built up by a lifetime of reading. Readers of essays in history bring to your writing expectations they have formed by reading many other books and articles about history. Don't disappoint them. Guide your own work by the following standards.

1. The historical essay has an argument.

We write essays about history to interpret for readers something we want them to know about the past. We provide both data—information from our sources—and our argument about what the facts mean.

A good historical essay quietly expresses the thrill of a writer's discovery. You cannot have that thrill yourself or convey it to others if you do nothing but repeat what others have said about your topic. Don't be content with telling a story others have told hundreds of times, the sort of story you might copy out of an encyclopedia whose aim is to give you the facts, the facts, and nothing but the facts. Find something puzzling in the evidence and try to solve it. Ask a question and try to answer it.

2. The good historical essay has a sharply focused and limited topic.

You can develop a thrill of discovery *only* if you limit your topic sufficiently to let you study the sources carefully and think about

13

them thoroughly. Find a topic you can manage in the time you have available.

Most unsuccessful history papers in my experience fall short because the writer has chosen a subject no one can possibly treat in the space and time available. An eighteen-year-old student of mine several years ago wanted to write on "A Psychoanalysis of Henry VIII" in seven pages. England's Henry VIII was a complicated man, as any one of his six wives and numerous mistresses might have testified. If a modern psychiatrist with degrees in medicine and psychotherapy put Henry on the couch and interviewed him day after day, two or three years would pass before the psychiatrist felt capable of making a judgment about Henry's character and motives. A student with no training in psychiatry and no knowledge of the thousands of pages written about this bizarre man cannot say anything worthwhile on so broad a topic.

Here is a lesson to brand in fire across any young historian's mind: If you try to do too much, you will not do anything. To write a good essay in history you must be sure that evidence is available, that you have had the time to study it carefully and repeatedly, and that you choose a topic on which you can say something worthwhile.

Some of my best students have written papers such as these: "A Study of the Prejudices against Blacks and Women in the 1911 Edition of the *Encyclopaedia Britannica*"; "Ten Years of Opinions by Historians on the Value of *The Age of Jackson* published by Arthur M. Schlesinger, Jr., in 1945"; "How a Confusion in Orders Caused the British Disaster in the Battles of Lexington and Concord on April 19, 1775."

Each of these topics was limited enough to allow the student writer to study the evidence carefully over several weeks, to consider problems in the sources, and to do several drafts of an essay.

3. Good papers in history come from primary sources.

Primary sources are the texts nearest to any subject of investigation; secondary sources are always written *about* primary sources. Primary sources for an essay about President Harry S. Truman would include letters Truman wrote throughout his life; secondary sources would include books and articles written about him, including the splendid biography written by David McCullough and called simply *Truman*. For a paper about Woodrow Wilson as historian, Wilson's *A History of the American People* is a primary source, as are the class notes he used for his lectures at Bryn Mawr and Princeton when he was a college teacher. Secondary sources would be some of the essays historian Arthur S. Link wrote about Wilson's writing about history.

The most common primary sources are written documents. My student who wanted to examine attitudes towards blacks and women in the 1911 Edition of the *Encyclopaedia Britannica* had read an article in *The New Yorker* magazine about this famous edition, noted for its clear writing and careful drawings illustrating the engineering wonders of the day. The *New Yorker* article commented on the encyclopedia's racist assumptions. My student wanted to see for herself not only what the 1911 edition said about race but how it treated women. She studied articles on the "Negro," on Africa, and on various issues relating to women, and she noted that the editors had included scarcely any articles on famous women in history. The *New Yorker* article about the encyclopedia was a secondary source; the primary source was the encyclopedia itself, and it was available in several sets in our university libraries.

But primary sources can also include photographs, paintings, sculpture, architecture, oral interviews, statistical tables, and even geography. While nearly all the clothes and fabric from Greek, Roman, and medieval times have been destroyed, we can get a fairly good idea of the history of fashion by looking at sculpture and painting left over from those years.

Never forget the power of the interview in writing about history. If you write about a particular antiwar demonstration during the Vietnam war, don't rely solely on newspaper accounts or on books about those demonstrations. Find some participants and ask them as many questions as you can. What did they do? What did others do? Why did they do these things? What happened?

4. Write your history paper in the same spirit that you would tell a good story.

As we said in the introduction, a good story begins with something out of balance, some tension to be resolved or explained. Or you can say that a good story begins with a problem. Here is a history beginning that works:

> "The whole affair was mismanaged from first to last." So wrote British Lieutenant John Barker in his diary after he survived the battles of Lexington and Concord on the first day of fighting in the American Revolution. Why did well-trained professional British sol-

diers meet with such a disastrous defeat at the hands of disorganized American farmers called "minute men"? Barker had one answer—the ineptitude of his own British commanders.

The writer gets to the point quickly by quoting Barker and revealing a tension that we want to see resolved. Seeing the quotation, we ask questions: "How was the affair mismanaged?" "Was Barker right?" "How could the British have avoided defeat that day?" The beginning puts various elements together, reveals tension, makes us ask questions, and proceeds.

You can just as well begin a history paper by considering an intellectual problem.

The 1911 edition of the *Encyclopaedia Britannica* reflects the racial attitudes of white Europeans and Americans at the time. Peoples of color—especially black Africans and others of African descent—are considered inferior, an idea that justified European and American imperialism with its assumption that the white powers were obligated to lift these inferior people closer to the level of white civilization. In addition the 1911 edition assumes the inferiority of women, leaving white European and American males in charge of the destiny of the world.

Both these beginnings introduce a problem—something out of order—at the very start of the essay. We then read on to see how the problem is resolved or explained. The problem may be in deciding precisely what happened. The puzzle may lie in tracing cause and effect, or in the influence one event had on another, or in the different interpretations historians have given of various events. (History has its own history; the books historians write are often conditioned by the biases of their times.)

The main quality of a story is that it makes us relive the experience that it describes. We feel cheated and probably angry standing in line to be admitted to a mystery movie if a kid coming out of the theatre shouts at us, "The girl friend did it." We say to friends who have seen a movie we plan to see, "Don't tell me how it ends." We want to live through the experience for ourselves. A good writer creates the experience of living through events or of living through a step-by-step interpretation of those events. In writing about the history of ideas, historians tell the story of how thinkers in the past have come to their conclusions, allowing readers to experience this process of discovery.

Any good piece of writing guides us through a process, providing information that lets us follow the writer's lead and arrive finally at the climax, where everything comes together. This does not mean that writers of history papers should necessarily give us surprise endings. Inexerpienced writers often fall into the temptation of withholding information or otherwise distracting us to prevent readers from guessing where they are going. Such tactics are annoying, and professional historians do not use them. The climax in a history paper is usually a place where the last block of information is fitted in place and the writer's case is proved as well as the writer's knowledge permits. Then the paper ends at the climax because once the case is proved, there is no point in continuing, except perhaps to tell what happened to the participants in events or to discuss their later influence.

5. Get to the point quickly.

A good essay sets the scene quickly, reveals a tension to be resolved, and sets out in the direction of a solution. Some writers take so long to introduce their essays that readers lose interest before they get to the writer's real beginning. The writers shovel out piles of background information. Or we may get an account of previous scholarship, flung at us like a fist full of sand to prove that the writer has studied the issue. Or we may get some sort of moral justification for the topic with this as an implied reason: "I am writing this paper to produce a better world and to prove that I am on the right side of things." The best writers have something important to say and start saying it quickly. Within two paragraphs of the beginning, your readers should understand why you have written your essay.

Here is a good beginning to a paper about history. See how quickly the author gets to the point:

> For thirty years J. E. Neale's portrait of the Elizabethan parliaments was the stuff of textbooks. Highly political and bedeviled by puritanical porto-bolsheviks, the Virgin Queen's parliaments were painted as the nursery in which the modern parliamentary system, characterized by an organized Opposition, was born. In the last decade, however, Neale's interpretations have been challenged and overturned, making obsolete most of the histories of Elizabethan England available to students. The purpose of this article is to assess the new research on Elizabethan parliaments, to summarize what we now know about the role Parliament played in governing England, and to suggest what remains to be done.[1]

[1]Norman L. Jones, "Parliament and the Governance of Elizabethan England: A Review," *Albion*, Fall 1987, p. 327.

Here in one paragraph the author presents the problem and tells us what he is going to do about it. He presents information; we know that he will develop some ideas that arise from what he gives us here. The more striking the information at the beginning, the larger the interest that may be provoked among readers.

Once you have begun, don't digress. Stick to the point. Be sure everything in your paper serves your main purpose, and be sure your readers understand the relation to the main purpose of everything you include. Never treat an essay as an exam requiring you to tell everything you know. The purpose of an essay is to make a point about what you know, not merely to pour out facts as if you were dumping the contents of a can onto a tabletop.

6. Write a good title for your paper.

A sharp title, perhaps supplemented by a subtitle, informs your reader and helps keep you on track as you write. Many popular magazines publish articles on historical subjects; they usually also provide subtitles. Historians writing for professional journals often use a colon to achieve the effect of a subtitle. Here is the title of an influential article by Hanna Holborn Gray in the 1963 *Journal of the History of Ideas:*

Renaissance Humanism: The Pursuit of Eloquence

Readers know immediately that the article is to be about Renaissance humanism, defined here as "the pursuit of eloquence." A title in the summer 1987 issue of *Albion,* a journal devoted to British history, is, "Evangelical Thought: John Wesley and Jonathan Edwards." We know at once that the author intends to study evangelical thought as it was expressed by John Wesley and Jonathan Edwards, who led great religious revivals at the same time, Wesley in England and Edwards in America. Go from a clear title to the purpose of your paper as quickly as you can. Titles, subtitles, and opening paragraphs should fit together as a unit.

Here is an essay in which the beginning is nicely fitted to a good title. Note the title, the subtitle, and the first two paragraphs.

The Bubonic Plague

A bacterial disease carried by fleas that feed on rats, it has afflicted human beings for more than 1,000 years. The factors responsible for its alternate rise and fall remain a mystery.

In the year 1346 Europe, northern Africa and nearer parts of the Middle East had a total population of approximately 100 million people. In the course of the next few years a fourth of them died, victims of a new and terrifying illness that spread throughout the area, killing most of those unfortunate enough to catch it. The disease put an end to the population rise that had marked the evolution of medieval society: within four years Europe alone suffered a loss of roughly 20 million people.

The disease responsible for such grim statistics was the bubonic plague, and this particular outbreak, lasting from 1346 to 1352, was known as the Great Dying or the Great Pestilence. Later it was appropriately referred to as the Black Death, a name that has come down through history. Although the effects of the Black Death may have been particularly catastrophic, striking as it did after a long period in which the disease had been unknown in the West, this was not the first time the plague had ravaged Europe. Some 800 years earlier, during the reign of the emperor Justinian in the sixth century, there was an epidemic of similar proportions. There were also repeated, if less widespread, epidemics in the two centuries following the plague of Justinian's time, and for four centuries after the Black Death. The disease has undergone a precipitous decline since that time, but it still occurs sporadically in various parts of the world today, including the U.S.[2]

The title interests anybody who has heard of the bubonic plague. The first paragraph's information that 20 million people died in a plague is both appalling and fascinating. We want to know more. We learn in the second paragraph that the subject of this essay will be a history of outbreaks of the Black Death. We are hooked.

Keep revising your beginning until it is direct, concise, and interesting. Start with the puzzle that excited your curiosity about the subject and made you think this topic would generate a good paper. If you are interested in something, you can make your readers interested in it, too.

7. Build your essay step by step on evidence.

You must give readers reasons to believe your story. That means that you have to know something and that your readers must recognize you as an authority for the essay you present to them. You can't

[2]Colin McEvedy, "The Bubonic Plague," *Scientific American,* February 1988, p. 118.

write history off the top of your head, and you can't parade your opinions unless you support them. Nobody cares about your opinions if you don't know anything or if you don't take the trouble to tell us what you do know.

Writing about history is much like proving a case in a court of law. A good lawyer does not stand before a jury and say, "My friends, I firmly believe my client is innocent. You must believe he is innocent because I believe he is innocent. I feel totally convinced that he is innocent. You may think he is guilty. I disagree. I feel in my bones that he is innocent. And I want you to rule that he is not guilty because in my opinion he is not guilty. Take my word for it."

Clients with such lawyers should prepare themselves to spend a long time away from home in undesirable company. A bad lawyer may repeat himself again and again. He may shout or weep or whisper or swear to the sincerity of his feelings. But the jury will not believe him unless he can produce some evidence.

So it is with the historical essay. Your readers are judge and jury. You are the lawyer arguing your case. It's all very well if your readers think you are sincere or high-minded or even eloquent; it's much more important that you convince them that you are right. To do that you must command your evidence and present it clearly and carefully.

What is evidence? The issue is more complicated than it may seem at first glance. Evidence is detailed factual information from primary and secondary sources. You must sift through those sources, decide what is reliable and what is not, and decide then how you will use those sources in your work. Serious journalists follow a rule that historians should use, too: When you make a generalization, immediately support it by quoting, summarizing, or otherwise alluding to a source. Generalizations are unconvincing without the help of specific information to give them content.

Historians fit their evidence together to create a story, an explanation, or an argument. To have evidence at their command, they spend days in libraries, in museums, or wherever sources of evidence are to be found. You cannot manufacture evidence out of thin air; you have to look for it. And when you find it you have to study it until you know it almost by heart. If you make a careless summary of your evidence and get it wrong, you will lose the respect of knowledgeable readers.

Evidence is everywhere. Sometimes people make spectacular discoveries of lost or forgotten documents. The discovery of the journals kept by James Boswell, the eighteenth-century companion and biographer of Samuel Johnson, was a remarkable event. They turned up in a Scottish castle where they had been scattered about like so much waste paper. The capture and opening of German archives following World War II has been an even more momentous discovery, allowing us now to trace German political and military policy through this century. The Freedom of Information Act has opened many FBI and other goverment files that were long secret, and much historical information has been gained from this source. The collapse of the Soviet Union has opened vast archives to scholars. Historians studying those archives one piece at a time will eventually better understand what happened during decades of paranoid secrecy in the former USSR.

The papers of important men and women in history are often printed and published in great editions. I worked for years on the *Yale Edition of the Complete Works of St. Thomas More* published by Yale University Press. Now every student of Thomas More can go to this edition. The papers of American presidents are being steadily published by universities, the work supported by large federal grants. The papers of Woodrow Wilson have been published by Princeton University Press in sixty-eight large volumes. The papers of Andrew Johnson are appearing slowly from the University of Tennessee Press. Many college libraries have these and other presidential papers or can get them on interlibrary loan.

The letters and papers of men and women, famous and obscure, make fascinating records of their times, and many collections have been published from the classical age to the present. Ralph Waldo Emerson's voluminous journal is in print. The letters of Desiderius Erasmus are being published in the English translation in dozens of volumes at the University of Toronto Press.

Sources of local history abound in courthouses, old newspapers (often preserved on microfilm), diaries, letters, tax records, city directories, the recollections of older people, and myriads of other places.

I worked on a newspaper afternoons when I was studying journalism at the University of Tennessee. I wrote a column about the history of our county, interviewing older people and looking at old records wherever I found them. Two elderly women allowed me to use the diary of their father, sheriff of our county in 1887 at the time of the last public hanging on our courthouse lawn. The man hanged was named Andrew Taylor, and he had not only robbed a train but had also shot the engineer and driven the train into our town before making his getaway on horseback. The sheriff went after him with a posse, captured him in a cave, and brought him back for trial and execution. I was able to find newspaper files from that time that gave me yet another view of the trial, and I even found a very old man living in a cockroach-infested rented room who as a child had seen Andy Taylor bring the train into the railroad station and gallop away. I wrote a story for the newspaper that would have done just as well in a history class.

Historians love evidence. They love old things. They immerse themselves in evidence, see its patterns, and write about them. To write a good paper without studying evidence is like trying to ride a bicycle without wheels.

8. Document your sources.

Formal essays in history document their sources by means of footnotes, endnotes, or attributions written into the text. Readers want to know where you got your facts. (Later in this book we'll discuss various ways of documenting sources.) You gain authority for your own work if you demonstrate that you are familiar with the primary sources and the work of others who have studied the same material.

Documenting sources is the best way to avoid plagiarism. It is dishonest to take either facts or interpretations from others without letting readers know that you have done so *unless* those facts are common knowledge. Plagiarism is the act of presenting the thoughts or words of others as your own; it constitutes the ultimate dishonesty in writing. Always put material you copy from your sources in quotation marks if you use it word for word in your essay as you found it in the sources. Always tell your readers when you are summarizing or paraphrasing a source. Always give credit to the ideas you get from someone else, even if you express those ideas in your own words.

9. Historical essays are written dispassionately.

Do not choke your prose with your emotions. We identify with the people and the times we are writing about; that is a major reason we find history interesting. Often we judge people in the past, deciding whether they were villains or heroes, or a little of both. The best way to convey those judgments is to tell what these people did or said. You don't have to prove that you are on the side of the angels; you can trust your reader. If characters you describe did terrible things, readers can see the evil if you give them the details. If the characters did noble things, your readers can see that, too. Describing the British retreat from Concord and Lexington on April 19, 1775, historian Louis Birnbaum lets the facts speak for themselves:

> The mood of the British soldiers was murderous. They surged around houses along the route, instantly killing anyone found inside. Some of the regulars looted whatever they could find, and some were killed while looting by Minutemen who had concealed themselves in the houses. Houses with fires in the hearth were burned down simply by spreading the embers about. Generally, those homes without fires on the hearth escaped destruction because it was too time-consuming to start a fire with steel and flint. As the column approached Menotomy, the 23rd Regiment was relieved of rear-guard duty by the marine battalion. Colonial fire reached a bloody crescendo in Menotomy, and again British troops rushed house after house, killing everyone found inside, including an invalid named Jason Russell.[3]

The author could have said, "The criminal and bloodthirsty British soldiers acted horribly in what they did to these poor, innocent people," or "So does war bring out the worst in us," or, "The wicked British soldiers who were killed in the act of looting houses got what they deserved." But readers don't need such coercive comments, and they often resent them. If you have presented the details, you can trust your readers to have the right reactions. You waste time and become a little absurd if you preach at them.

10. A historical essay should include original thoughts of the author; it should not be a rehash of the thoughts of others.

Essays are examples of reasoning. The most respected essays demonstrate an author carefully setting things in order and making sense of them. Don't disappoint your readers by telling them only

[3]Louis Birnbaum, *Red Dawn at Lexington,* Boston, Houghton Mifflin, 1986, p. 184.

what other people have said about your subject. Try to show them that by reading your work they will learn something new or see old knowledge in a new light, one that you have shed on the subject by your own study and thinking.

One of the saddest things I find about teaching is the conviction of too many of my students that they have nothing fresh and interesting to say about their topics. They do not trust themselves. They cannot express a thought unless they have read it somewhere else.

One reason for this lack of confidence is that some students insist on writing about large, general topics that other people have written about hundreds of times. Only a little searching will turn up evidence for topics that have seldom been written about. Such evidence exists in every college library. If you take the time to look, you too can turn up new information and shape papers that are new and original.

Even if you do not find completely new facts, you can think carefully about the facts at your disposal and come up with something fresh and interesting. You can see new relations. You can see causes and effects that others may have missed. You may reflect on motives and influences. You may spot places where some sources are silent. You can present your own conclusions, which have the weight of authority behind them.

Don't write a paper in the spirit that a child builds a model plane bought in a kit from a hobby shop. The child sticks together parts that someone else has designed until she produces a model that looks like the picture on the box. Some students go to the library looking for information on a broad subject like the beginnings of the Civil War, and take a piece of information here and another piece there. They stick it all together without contributing anything of their own except manual dexterity. They retell a story that has been told thousands of times, and they don't present a thought that they have not read elsewhere.

Do not be happy until you can shape a story that cannot be read in every encyclopedia or textbook on the field.

11. Always consider your audience.

No one can write to please or interest every possible reader. Different articles are intended for different audiences. Every beginning history student should spend a few hours in the library looking at the different periodicals devoted to history. It is fairly easy to spot publications devoted to a popular audience and those devoted to specialists. The *American Historical Review,* the official journal of the

American Historical Association, is devoted to specialists—usually professors of history—who know the subject fairly well. *American Heritage* and *History Today* are aimed at readers with an educated interest in history who are not necessarily specialists, but these publications are reliable and interesting. Study these various journals and analyze their differences. You may then begin to see how different the intended audiences may be.

Consider what your intended audience knows. For most history courses, you should write for your teacher and for other students who have an interest in the subject but who may not be specialists in the field. Define important terms. Give enough information to provide a context for your essay. Say something about your sources, but don't get lost in background information in other facts that you expect edu-

If you write an interpretation of Martin Luther King, Jr.'s *Letter from Birmingham Jail* in 1965, you will bore readers and even offend them if you write as if they have never heard of Martin Luther King, Jr., so that you assume you must first tell them the whole story of his life before you get to your discussion of the text. To set a context for an essay on the subject, you need to say only that Dr. King had been jailed for his efforts to organize demonstrations against segregation in Birmingham and that a group of white Alabama clergymen had taken out an advertisement in a newspaper condemning his activities and asking him to stop. That statement, coming somewhere near the beginning of your essay, will set a context to help readers remember some of the details of how Dr. King came to write the work.

No writer can be entirely sure what an audience knows or does not know. Just as we convey to our readers an "implied author," so we always write with an implied reader in mind, someone we think may read this work. Think of yourself as a reader and consider the sort of thing you might read and believe. With those thoughts in mind, write for the curious, interested person you think you are.

I tell my students that they should write their essays so fully that if their roommates picked up the essay they would be able to read it in the same way that they can read an article in a serious magazine. The essay should be complete in itself. The important terms should be defined, every person quoted or mentioned in the essay should be identified, and all the necessary information should be included. I like to think of a roommate picking up an essay, beginning to read, and not being able to stop until he or she has finished the piece.

12. An honest essay takes contrary evidence into account.

Good historians try to tell the truth about what happened. If you study any issue long enough and carefully enough, you will form opinions about it. You will think you know why something happened, or you will suppose that you understand a personality clearly. Yet the evidence in history seldom stacks up entirely on one side of an issue, especially in the more interesting problems about the past. Different parts of the evidence contradict each other; using your own judgements about it all means that you must face such contradictions squarely. If you do not, knowledgeable readers will think you are careless, incompetent, or even dishonest.

President Woodrow Wilson is a hero to many liberals today, including many historians of an older generation. He conceived the idea of the League of Nations, the failed ancestor to the present United Nations, and he advocated a peace without vengeance after the horrors of World War I. Yet President Wilson treated black Americans as inferior, did not want them to have the vote in the South, and instituted segregation in the Federal Civil Service. How do we deal with this contradictory evidence? Given the abundant evidence of Wilson's racial attitudes in the Princeton Edition of his papers, it is careless and even dishonest to portray him as a great liberal hero without acknowledging this other side to his character and his political record.

Different historians interpret the same facts in very different ways. In highly controversial issues, you must take into account views that oppose your own. If, for example, you should argue that Robert E. Lee was responsible for the Confederate defeat at the Battle of Gettysburg, you must consider the argument of a number of historians that the blame should be laid at the feet of General James Longstreet, one of Lee's subordinates. You may still argue that Lee was the major cause of the defeat (although you should also remember that the Union army had something to do with it). You do not weaken your case by recognizing opposing views: You strengthen your own argument by showing readers that you know your facts—even those facts that seem to contradict your argument. They will believe you if you deal with those contradictions honestly, but they will not believe if you pretend that the contradictions do not exist. If you give informed readers the impression that you are hiding information, you lose them on the spot. This advice translates into a simple principle:

Be honest. Nothing turns readers off so quickly as to suppose that the writer is not being fair with the facts.

13. Essays use standard English and observe the common conventions of writing.

Sometimes student writers feel abused when teachers require them to spell words correctly, to use correct grammar and punctuation, and to proofread their papers. But it is a terrible distraction to try to read a paper that does not observe the conventions. Readers should be paying attention to what a writer says. They should not be asking themselves questions like these: "Is that word spelled correctly?" "Why has he not put a comma here?" "Why has he used this word?" Reading is hard work, especially when the material is dense or complicated, as it often is in history courses. A careless attitude toward the conventions may not bother writers because they at least think they know what they want to say, but it throws readers off.

Students who complain when teachers enforce the conventions do themselves a great disservice. In the world beyond college, few things about your writing will be more harshly judged than careless disregard for the conventions. We all would like to believe that our ideas are so compelling that no one can resist them, no matter how sloppily we write. Readers we are trying to impress in a job application or in a report or letter will judge otherwise. Never hand in a paper without proofreading it carefully. Read it over and over to find any misspelled words, lapses in grammar, typos, and places where you may have inadvertently left out a word (a common error in these days of writing with the computer).

14. Let your first and last paragraphs mirror each other.

The first and the last paragraphs of a good essay reflect some of the same words and thoughts. You can read these paragraphs and have a pretty good idea of what the intervening essay is about. An essay is somewhat like a snake biting its tail: The end always comes back to the beginning. You can see that mirroring of first and last paragraphs in the essay on fashion by Mary Louise Roberts quoted in the introduction of this book.

The end should not come back to the beginning in a mechanical way. You should not begin an essay by saying, "In this essay I am going to do this, this, and this," and you should not conclude by saying, "In this essay I have done this, this, and this." Such beginnings and endings are boring. You should try to begin and end in a more interesting way. In whatever way you begin, your first and last paragraphs should demonstrate some common words and thoughts.

These are the principles of good essays about history. Keep them in mind as you write your own.

2

Thinking about History

Writing history involves a special way of thinking. The past in all its complexity cannot be recaptured like an instant replay when we're watching football or baseball on television. Real life has no instant replay. History does not repeat itself. The stuff of history—human experience—moves ceaselessly, changing endlessly in a process so complicated that it is like a turning kaleidoscope that never makes the same pattern twice.

The present is different from the past. We have to recognize that difference before we can think historically. To write history, then, means making an effort to tell the story of the past in language that makes sense to readers in the present. But the very effort to make sense to readers in the present may distort the story. It is all a very difficult business!

The problems of history resemble the problems of memory. What were you doing a year ago today? If you keep an appointment book, you can look in it and find the names of people you saw that day. But what did you say when you saw them? If you keep a journal, you have a better record. But the journal does not tell you everything. Someone says to you, "I remember when we sat on the beach at Pawley's Island, South Carolina, year before last in August and talked about Elvis Presley's death." "Oh," you may say, "I thought that was three years ago in Charleston."

All our knowledge of history comes from sources. As I have said already, the sources themselves have been conditioned by when they were created, and we are conditioned by our own times in how we read sources from the past. Legends of the saints told in the Middle Ages are filled with miraculous happenings. St. Denis was said to have been beheaded in Paris while preaching to the pagan Gauls; he walked with his head in his hands to the site that later became the monastery of St. Denis outside of the city and set his head down there to mark the place where he should be buried. The kings of France were later buried in the monastery church built on the site. A statue of the saint, holding his head in his hands, is now on the front of Notre Dame Cathedral in Paris.

Most of us do not believe that people can walk around holding their heads in their hands. We respect this story only as a charming tale, not literal truth. For one thing, it was a good way for the bishops of Paris to emphasize the importance of their city and the truth of the orthodox Christian theology they professed against unorthodox beliefs held by many of the Germanic invaders of the old Roman empire. The miracle certified truth. So in our nicely modern perceptions of the past, we find a rational explanation for the story and congratulate ourselves for our reasonableness.

But what happens to nice, reasonable explanations when we come to a modern phenomenon such as Adolf Hitler? Why did Hitler go to war in 1939? He seemed to have everything Germany could want in Europe. France, Britain, and even the Soviet Union cowered before him and did everything they could to prove to him that they did not want to fight. He had been a soldier himself in World War I and knew the horrors of modern warfare and mass destruction. Did he go to war because he miscalculated? Or did he go to war because he loved war and wanted war no matter what peace terms the allies were willing to give him and no matter what price he and Germany had to pay?

Historians have lined up on both sides of this question. The theory that he simply miscalculated arises in part because rational people—among them university historians—cannot believe that anyone would deliberately lead his people into the devastation of modern war. Just as we cannot believe that St. Denis walked across Paris carrying his severed head in his hands, we cannot believe that even Hitler would be so irrational as to seek the war that came.

Yet we also recognize in this post-Freudian world that human motives are complex, mysterious, and often absurd. Many people do crazy and destructive things for no reason that we can see. All this is to say that the study of history involves us in modes of thought common in daily life. We weigh evidence, deciding what to believe and what not. We interpret evidence. We tell stories about what happened. We try to discover what it all means—and what it means to be a human being.

We begin to think creatively in the study of history by learning how to ask questions of our sources. In the rest of this chapter you will find some ways to pose these questions with the aim of wringing out of a text information and ideas that will help you write original and interesting papers.

QUESTIONING YOUR SOURCES

I have said that good papers in history are built on primary sources. My heart sinks when I get a paper whose major sources are *Time* or *Newsweek*, or *U.S. News and World Report* or *The New York Times*. These are all good journals, but it is laziness for a student writer to make them the most important sources of information for a history essay. Go to the primary sources.

Yes, you should consult secondary sources to develop some background for your paper. Go to the reference room of your library and read articles in many different encyclopedias about your subjects. Read articles in news magazines. Look up important words in dictionaries to be sure you understand how they are used by people you write about. Ask reference librarians where to look for general information on your subject. This overview will give you a feel for your subject and for the general state of knowledge about it. The time you spend now doing this preliminary reading will save you much time later as you work with your evidence.

At some moment, however, you must go to primary sources and study them thoroughly. If you want to write a paper on Woodrow Wilson's racial attitudes, go to the Wilson papers and use the index in each volume to direct you to Wilson's thoughts on various subjects related to your topic.

Read with the journalistic questions in mind—who, what, where, when, and why. It is a good idea to jot those questions down in your notes and try to answer them briefly as you read. They will help you sort things out and organize your approach to the subject. The questions correspond to a natural and almost universal way that literate people respond to information. When you approach any body of evidence or any issue in history, you can ask who the people involved were, what happened, when it happened, where it happened, and why it happened. The answers may overlap. It may be impossible to separate a *what* question from a *why* question. To explain what happened is sometimes to explain why it happened. We can scarcely separate a *who* question from a *what* question; to talk about someone is to discuss what that person did.

The fact that the questions overlap is the very reason journalists use them. A complex event is like an elaborate tapestry tightly woven of many different-colored threads. The threads are distinct, but they are difficult to sort out. The journalistic questions help us keep our eyes on this or that important thread so we can see how it contributes to the whole. They help us analyze human actions.

To analyze means to "break down," to separate into parts. Analysis of human events helps us to see them in subtly different ways important to writing or reading about history or any other discipline. For example, the question, "Who committed the murder?" combines a *who* and a *what* since what happened—the murder—calls up the question, "Who did it?" Yet they are different questions.

In police investigations (and in mystery stories), detectives look for motives. Why was the murder committed? Suspicion falls on those people who had some reason to kill the victim. Yet to establish a motive is not to prove that the person with a clear motive was the killer. The victim may have had many enemies. Racial segregation in the federal civil service—including the United States Post Office—came about during the administration of President Woodrow Wilson shortly after he took office in 1913. That is what happened. But who was responsible? Who influenced Wilson? Who was affected? Who protested? Why was segregation installed? When was it installed? Where was it carried out? The emphasis we place on this or that journalistic question may determine the approach we take to writing an essay about a historical event. We might write one essay about Woodrow Wilson's racial attitudes, and another quite different essay on segregation in the federal civil service and its relation to segregation policies in state and local governments in America.

The journalistic questions can help you work through writer's block. All of us experience writer's block at one time or another. We can't get started, or we can't continue, or we can't finish. If you write out the journalistic questions and various answers to them, you can give your mind a little push that starts an engine going in your work. *Writing stimulates the mind; almost any process that gives you a chance to write about the topic of your essay will inspire your mind with thoughts you could not have had if you had not started writing first.*

Remember that each journalistic question can be posed in many different ways. There is not one *who* question or *what* question or one *why* question. There may be dozens. Ask as many of them as you can. Push your mind.

Who was Martin Luther? Whom did he oppose? Who opposed him? Who protected him? Who supported him? Who wrote about him? Who were his associates? What did he do? What did he believe? What did he want? What did his opponents do? What did his supporters do? What did his associates do? What did indifferent Germans do? Why did he do these things? Why did he gather such a following? Why was he not put to death? Why did supporters rally to his side? Why did enemies hate and fear him? When did he live? When did he arrive at the ideas that made him break with the Catholic Church? When did he stop believing in purgatory? When did he stop believing in a burning hell? When did he start believing that the souls of the dead remained asleep until the day of judgment? When did he realize that he had started a new movement rather than a reform of the Catholic Church? When did he think the world would end? When did he sanction armed resistance to Catholic authorities? Where did he live? Where did he have the greatest influence? Where did he have the least influence? Where have his works been most studied? Where have most biographies about him appeared? Where did Luther travel in his life?

As you ask these questions, jotting down brief answers—or noting that you don't know the answers—you suggest many different topics, more than you can possibly write about in one well-focused paper. You will begin to see relations between some of your questions. For example, you may push yourself to ask a dozen or more *where* questions. That effort may make you ask, "Where did Luther travel in his life?" Some scholars have argued that because Luther left the German lands only once in his life and after 1522 seldom left the little town of Wittenberg, he did not have to meet the sort of stern questioning from independent minds that might have made him modify his assertions or resolve some of the contradictions in his thought. Since his world was relatively enclosed, he could dominate his own small circle so much that he rarely changed his mind in response to arguments by colleagues. Here a *what* question and a *where* question and perhaps a *why* question are all linked.

Jot down as many *what* questions as you can think of, even if some of them seem frivolous. Then ask as many *why* questions as possible, and so on. The questions shape your thinking. Asking one helps you ask another, and you may discover that almost without knowing how it happened, you have come on a question that may make a good subject for a paper. Now let's look at the questions one by one.

Who?

When we ask the question "who?" we often seek biographical information. Who exactly was Woodrow Wilson? Who were his parents? Who were his early influences? Who were his friends? Who became his enemies? The *who* question makes us think of character. What kind of person was Woodrow Wilson? What did people who knew him say about him? A character sketch—drawn from several sources, expressing good and bad, including consistencies and contradictions—can make an excellent history paper. It would be especially interesting to see where friends and enemies agreed on qualities of his personality.

You can always write about the divergent opinions of historians about a historical figure, because good historians answer the *who* question in different ways; those different views are worth studying and comparing.

The *who* question makes us think about responsibility. Who was most responsible for the outbreak of World War I? Who was the most effective leader in the civil rights movement of the 1950s and 1960s? Who has been most influential in gaining civil rights for women in recent years? The *who* question may make us think of who was first in performing some act. Who first understood what was required to make an airplane fly? Who first thought that a Communist society might solve most social problems? Who were the first Communists to reject the terrorism of Joseph Stalin in Russia? Who was the first person killed in a car crash? Who first flew across the Atlantic Ocean? Who made the first practical tin can? Who invented dynamite? Who invented the paper towel? Who developed the first workable technique for cleaning woolen clothes? Who invented modern lipstick?

The *who* question may also turn our attention to those affected by various events in history. Who died in the medieval plague called the Black Death, the rich or the poor or both? Who has been most helped by federal civil rights legislation? Who has been least helped? Who is most likely to be influenced by newspaper editorials? Who are the most common victims of drug abuse? Who were the supposed beneficiaries of William Jennings Bryan's campaign for the free coinage of silver when he ran as the Democratic nominee for the presidency in 1896? Who was most helped and who was most harmed by the Western railroads built in the nineteenth century?

Sometimes the *who* question will help us satisfy simple curiosity. Who knew about the planning of the Watergate burglary in 1972?

Who was involved in the English Bloomsbury group of writers early in this century? Who were the people most interested in passing a Prohibition amendment to the United States Constitution? Who were women writers in colonial America?

What?

The what question may involve weeding out the legends and misunderstandings to see what *really* happened. Deciding what happened is difficult—a matter of putting together bits and pieces of evidence to construct a mosaic. As I have said, our constructions of the past always have gaps. *What* questions may involve the historian in thinking much like a detective. What happened the night Luther died on February 18, 1546? Did he have a chance to make a pious exit in the arms of his friends uttering brave and faithful last words? Or did he die in his sleep? Both stories were told by people at the time. We can only infer which story is more plausible.

What happened at the Lexington Common in Massachusetts early in the morning of April 19, 1775, when British soldiers of the "King's Own" Regiment faced a ragged line of American colonials? The sources are immensely confused and contradictory.

Another *what* question asks, "What does this mean?" How we use words influences how we think about our evidence and what judgments we make about it. Words change their meaning, and yet they often carry forward certain connnotations. Always try to understand words from the past as people in the past used them. Don't confuse past understandings with present ones. In the nineteenth century the word *liberal* was used in England to describe businessmen who wanted to make a place for themselves in a country that had been dominated by an aristocracy with its power based on land holding. The liberals were capitalists who thought government ought to keep its hands off business. Most liberals believed that the economy ran by implacable laws of supply and demand and that any effort to help working people interfered with those laws and was bound to lead to catastrophe.

In the twentieth century the word *liberal* has been used in America to describe those who want government to hold the balance of power between the strong and the weak, and the rich and the poor, and to ensure that the rich and the powerful do not trample on the weak. What relation exists between the use of the words in these two seemingly radically different ways? The main similarity is in the root meaning of the word *liberal,* which comes from a Latin word meaning "liberty." Liberals in both the nineteenth and twentieth centuries have advocated liberty for citizens. Nineteenth-century liberals wanted to create liberty for the business classes who suffered under the restrictions of aristocratic custom. Twentieth-century liberals have tried to create more liberty for the poor, including the liberty that comes from public education, with its recognition of talent and its opportunities for advancement.

Anyone writing about liberalism has to be sure to see both the similarities and the differences in the two uses of the word. Such problems arise throughout the study of history. Be on guard to keep yourself from reading today's definition into yesterday's words. Don't rely on simple dictionary definitions of words. Words are defined by their context in time and place, and you must be sure to understand that context.

Why?

Sometimes we know what happened. But why did it happen, and why did it have the influence that it did? These questions about cause and effect create an eternal fascination. Keep in mind several considerations about cause and effect:

1. Always distinguish between the precipitating cause and the background causes of a great event.

You might call the precipitating cause the triggering cause, the cause that sets events in motion. The background causes are those that build up and create the context within which the precipitating cause works.

Precipitating causes are often dramatic and fairly clear-cut; background causes are more difficult to sort out and often ambiguous. The precipitating cause of the Civil War was the bombardment and capture of Fort Sumter by the forces of South Carolina on April 12, 1861. Immediately afterwards Lincoln called for 75,000 volunteers to suppress the rebellion, and soon thereafter fighting began. No one would say that the incident in Charleston Harbor all by itself caused the

Civil War. Behind the events of that Friday morning were complex differences between North and South—slavery in the Southern states, different economies, different cultures, different values, different political philosophies, different religious expressions, different educational systems, different histories, and finally the 1860 election of President Lincoln, known to oppose the extension of slavery into territories west of the Mississippi River. These were the background causes of the war, and ever since, historians have been trying to sort them all out and tell a sensible story explaining why America's bloodiest war tore the country apart for four years.

Background causes offer rich possibilities for writing about the *why* of history. They allow writers opportunities for research, analysis, and conjecture. They often figure in serious newspaper reports trying to explain events that suddenly make headlines. When Arab demonstrators began provoking violence from the Israeli army in the winter of 1987–1988, newspapers rushed to write about the many years of conflict on what is called the West Bank of the Jordan River, land taken over by the Israelis in the 1967 war with the Arabs. In effect these newspaper reporters were trying to explain the triggering causes that provoked weeks of violence. Those triggering causes would not have provoked anything unless there had been something there to provoke. If you pull the trigger of an empty pistol, you get only a snap of the firing pin. The gun has to be loaded before the pistol will fire. Background causes are, in effect, the cartridge loaded in the gun that makes the trigger do something important.

Historians write books and articles on such subjects. Why did the religious fundamentalist controversy break out in America during and after the First World War? The precipitating cause may have been a series of little religious books called *The Fundamentals* published then. Why did those little books have such an audience? What was happening in America that made them popular? These *why* questions probe at background causes.

Precipitating or triggering causes can be worthwhile subjects in themselves. Exactly what happened at Fort Sumter or Pearl Harbor or during the Watergate scandal will make an interesting story, perhaps more complicated than we usually suppose. Part of the first story involves the reasons the incident at Fort Sumter in April 12, 1861, did precipitate war. Why was it that passions were so aroused on that particular day in that particular year? The *what* question and the *why* question come together—as they often do.

2. Remember that historical causation is complex.

It is almost always a mistake to lay too much responsibility for a happening on only one cause. Rebecca West in her remarkable book about Yugoslavia published in 1942, *Black Lamb, Grey Falcon,* tells in detail the story of the assassination of the Archduke Franz Ferdinand of Austria-Hungary in Serajevo on Sunday, June 28, 1914—the precipitating cause of World War I. The Archduke was heir to the throne of the Austro-Hungarian Empire. When the Archduke was murdered, leaders of the Empire decided they must punish Serbia, the country in the Balkans the Austrians believed responsible for the terrorists who killed Franz Ferdinand and his wife. Russia defended Serbia because Serbia was made up of Slavs, akin to the Slavs in Russia. Germany defended Austria against Russia. When the Archduke was shot to death, a chain of events was set dragging across Europe that pulled the Continent into war. West tells the story of the assassination in novelistic detail.

She also goes deeply into all the centuries of conflict between Austria and Serbia, the parent of the Yugoslav state that fell apart only recently. Her thick book tells a complex story of grievances that the two peoples built up against each other, culminating in the assassination and the subsequent war. By building up so many sources of friction, West shows how easy it was for the death of the Archduke to precipitate the war—and helps us understand a little better the bloody fighting between Serbs and Bosnians that went on through 1993.

Good historical writing considers many different but related causes for a great happening. The study of history helps us see how many different influences flow into the making of any great event. Causes in history are like the tributaries to a great river. While a bad historian sees only the main channel of the largest stream, a good historian looks at the entire watershed and tries to map the smaller streams that contribute to the whole.

Good historians see things in context—often a large context of people and events surrounding what they seek to describe. Thinking in context means that we try to sort out and weigh the relative importance of various causes when we consider any important happening. The sense of context is especially important today, when historians have discovered the masses, the common people who must follow if leaders are to lead.

Nineteenth-century historians thought that if we understood the personalities of leaders, we knew everything we needed to know about historical movements. If we wanted to understand what happened in England at the end of the sixteenth century, we studied the life and work of Queen Elizabeth. If we wanted to understand the American Revolution, we studied Thomas Jefferson, George Washington, and a pantheon of other great leaders.

But now we ask questions like these: What was happening to the English people under Queen Elizabeth I that caused her to be more tolerant of religious diversity than former English monarchs had been? The later Middle Ages witnessed dozens of rebellions by various working-class people clamoring for a better life: Why were these people aroused so often in this period? Why was such a small band of American colonists who wanted independence from Great Britain able to have such a large effect on the majority of their fellow citizens, who were either indifferent to independence or loyal to the old crown at the time of the American Revolution?

Such questions involve finding ways to look at mass culture and the lives of people who were often scarcely literate and left little writing behind. Since it is difficult to resurrect the life of the masses, the problem of answering the *why* questions of history becomes complex and uncertain. Its difficulties do not remove from historians the obligation to consider the problem.

3. Be cautious in your judgments.

Do not seek easy and simple causes for complex and difficult problems. Do not argue that the Roman Empire fell only because Romans were drinking water from lead pipes, that the South lost the Civil War only because Lee was defeated at Gettysburg, that the Reformation came only because Martin Luther protested papal policy in Germany, or that the American civil rights movement was all the work of the Reverend Martin Luther King, Jr. All these events were caused by many complex influences. We become foolish when we try to put too much responsibility onto one dramatic event or famous leader.

The caution should also extend to your judgments about motivation in history. We know that the Roman Emperor Constantine legalized Christian worship in the Roman Empire after about 313 A.D. Was he a sincere Christian or not? Or did he see that the Christians were numerous and possessed a strong organization that might help hold together his decaying Empire? Was he devout? Or was he cynical?

Some have said that he was entirely cynical; a more recent school has held that he was sincere in his profession although his understanding of Christianity was warped and vague. Each party brings evidence to support its conclusions.

We cannot know for certain what motivated Constantine. Even if we have a pretty good idea one way or another, we should not present our conclusions so vehemently or so intolerantly that we make it seem that our view is the only one possible given the evidence, especially when we know that there is much to be said for the other side—or for several other sides.

Questions of motivation arise in every branch of historical study. Why did Franklin Roosevelt not open the gates of America to Jews persecuted by the Nazis under Hitler in the 1930s? Why did Thomas More die? Why did Richard Nixon try to cover up the Watergate burglaries? Why did Ernest Hemingway write so often about bravery and courage? Why did city people in the late Roman Empire accept Christianity while most country people stayed with the old gods?

Some *why* questions may appear to have been answered: Agreement on them is almost complete. Yet an inquiring historian may look on the evidence again and find another answer. Of such stuff is revisionism in history made. Why did the South suffer so much poverty in the years after the Civil War? An earlier answer was "Reconstruction," the supposedly merciless exploitation of the South by carpetbaggers from the North. Now the prevailing opinion is that white Southerners themselves with their one-crop economy, their resolve to suppress black citizenship, and their unwillingness to support public education were responsible for many of their own difficulties.

I happen to be writing just now a book about Martin Luther. Everybody who has written in recent years about Luther takes seriously his claim that he was tormented by his fear of the wrath of God when he was a young monk in early sixteenth-century Germany. I asked myself this question: Why was Luther's fear of God's wrath so intense? I believe that most scholars have assumed that he was terrified of the fiery hell artists so often portrayed, with the damned souls writhing in eternal torment and regret. I discovered that Luther had very little to say about hell and in time rejected entirely the notion of a burning hell portrayed by artists. But he wrote hundreds of pages about death, and I have come to believe that Luther's fear of the wrath of God was in essence a fear of death and annihilation. I have, of course, worked out my answer to this question at some length and with abundant citations, and I must wait to see how my conclusions are judged by other scholars of the sixteenth century. My point here is that careful study of the evidence may turn up new possibilities about some questions that seem to have been answered.

When and Where?

When and *where* questions often illuminate tricky puzzles in history. Sometimes we know exactly when and where something happened. We know the moment the first Japanese bombs fell on Pearl Harbor, the moment Franklin Roosevelt died, and exactly where the Confederate charge reached its high watermark on the third day of the battle of Gettysburg. But asking when something happened in relation to something else can provide a fascinating topic of research. We don't know when Richard Nixon first learned that members of his White House staff were involved in the Watergate burglary of June 17, 1972. When did Israel leave Egypt in the Exodus that is described in the Bible? Several dates have been argued. Different dates mean different chronologies for Israel's relations with other nations in the region and for the development of Israel's history. When did volcanic eruptions destroy Minoan civilization on Crete? The question is related to the rise of power on the Greek mainland under states such as Athens and Sparta. When did Woodrow Wilson first express himself in opposition to the aspirations of American blacks? Was it an attitude thrust upon him by others when he became president, or had he opposed black progress before he entered politics?

Questions about where things happened can often be absorbing. No one knows exactly the location of the Rubicon River. Julius Caesar crossed it with his army in violation of a law of the Roman Republic that forbade the army from approaching too near the capital. But wherever it was, it is called something else today. We know that the Rubicon was in North Italy and that it formed the border between the Roman province known as Cisalpine Gaul and the Roman Republic itself, but we do not know which modern Italian river was then called the Rubicon. Deciding where the Rubicon was might help us understand how much warning the Roman Senate had when Caesar started with his troops toward the capital.

Where questions involve geography, and geography often makes *where* questions overlap with *why* questions. Where are the rivers of the Netherlands? The rivers of France? The rivers of Germany? Various historians have argued that the rivers of France and the Netherlands provided a natural unity to those countries, whereas the rivers of Germany flow in such a way as to cause Germany to remain disunited. Where did the Greeks live? A study of patterns of Greek settlement may reveal much about Greek culture in the classical age. Where did different ethnic groups settle when they came to America? Where has most fundamentalist literature been produced? Where did the working classes live in eighteenth-century London? Where were most of the factories that produced iron and steel in the United States at the outbreak of the Civil War? Where were the first railroads built? All these questions have important meanings for history, and they may provide topics for original research.

Any good historian will examine the geographical context of any study. Geography may not yield anything special for your particular study, but if you ask the questions, you may discover a door opening in your mind on a hitherto unimagined landscape of events and explanation. The Annales school of history in France has made geography one of its most fundamental concerns, asking such questions as how long it took to travel from one place to another in Europe, what the major trade routes were, where different crops were grown, what cities had the closest relations to one another, and so on. Bernard DeVoto—an American author who wrote several popular books on the settlement of the American West—collected maps, and loved to spread them out on the floor of his house to demonstrate some of his major theses about the western migration.

For all historians, a good topographical map showing the roads, rivers, mountains, passes, coasts, and location of towns remains an indispensable resource. How long did it take news to travel from place to place in the Europe of the Middle Ages or the Renaissance? That question involves the location of the roads and their condition. Look at a contour map, one that shows mountains and valleys, and you can understand many of the reasons for the outbreak of World War I in 1914 and the subsequent German invasion of France through then neutral Belgium. The same sort of map will provide some reasons for the continued disunity of Africa. While geography will not explain everything, it will often help you understand some things. I can understand why Luther succeeded in Wittenberg; I cannot imagine his reformation getting anywhere if he had been a monk in Paris with the same convictions.

The Use of Inference

In our discussion of the journalistic questions we have assumed the ability of the mind to *infer.* We manage our daily life by making inferences. In the morning we see low, dark clouds blowing across the sky. When we leave home, we take along an umbrella. Why? We have seen such clouds before, and they have often meant rain.

We infer by calling on past experience to interpret a present event or situation. We cannot always be certain that what we infer is true. Sometimes the black clouds blow away quickly, leaving the skies clear so that we grumpily lug around a useless umbrella and maybe a raincoat all day long. But without inference we would have to reinvent the world every morning.

Historians infer some of the answers to all the journalistic questions. We strive to make sense of a document, to decide exactly what it is and whether it is reliable, and to understand why it might have been written, when it might have been written, where, and by whom. We are not told, for example, who wrote many of the books of the Bible or when they were written or just why they may have been written. Fascinating articles appear from time to time in journals such as *Archaeology* or *The Journal of Biblical Literature* trying to fit together discoveries in Palestine with the Biblical texts to see how the two might be fitted into a coherent whole.

Coherence is the aim of inference. We try to fit everything together into a plausible whole. Here is a letter written by General Robert E. Lee, leader of the Confederate Army of Northern Virginia during the American Civil War. The letter was written to his wife, an invalid, on April 5, 1863, a scant three months before Lee's army was defeated at the battle of Gettysburg. Lee has been sick, and in the letter he describes his illness to his wife:

> Genl Stuart brought me this morning your letter of yesterday dear Mary. I am much better I think, in fact when the weather becomes so that I can ride out, I shall get quite well again. I am suffering with a bad cold as I told you, & was threatened the doctors thought with some malady which must be dreadful if it resembles its

name, but which I have forgotten. So they bundled me upon Monday last & brought me over to Mr. Yuby's where I have a comfortable room with Perry to attend to me. I have not been so very sick, though have suffered a good deal of pain in my chest, back, & arms. It came on in paroxysms, was quite sharp & seemed to be to be a mixture of your's & Agnes' diseases, from which I infer they are catching & that I fell a victim while in R[ichmond]. But they have passed off I hope, some fever remains, & I am enjoying the sensation of a complete saturation of my system with quinine. The doctors are very attentive & kind & have examined my lungs, my heart, circulation, &c. I believe they pronounce me tolerable sound. They have been tapping me all over like an old steam boiler before condemning it. I am about a mile from my camp & my handsome aids ride over with the papers after breakfast which I labour through by 3 p.m., when Mrs. Neal sends me some good soup or something else which is more to my taste than the doctors pills. I am in need of nothing.[1]

What illness did Lee have? Given the limited medical knowledge of his day, we can only infer. Was he describing a heart attack? Or was it, as Edwin B. Coddington, a historian of the battle of Gettysburg, suggested, "pericarditis," an inflamation of the chest cavity where the heart is located?[2] Lee died in 1870, apparently from a heart attack. Were the symptoms manifest earlier? Historian Kent Masterson-Brown, in describing Lee at Gettysburg, says, "Lee had been troubled with angina pectoris, and during the campaign he contracted a severe case of diarrhea."[3] Diarrhea can be a symptom of heart trouble. Angina pectoris is pain in or around the heart and in itself does not diagnose Lee's ills. Harry W. Pfanz dismisses Lee's ailment before Gettysburg as pericarditis brought on by a sore throat.[4] Did illness affect his conduct of the battle? The consensus seems to be in the nega-

---

[1]*The Wartime Letters of R. E. Lee,* eds. Clifford Dowdey and Louis H. Manarin, New York, Bramhall House, 1961, pp. 427–428.

[2]Edward B. Coddington, *The Gettysburg Campaign: A Study in Command,* New York, Scribner's, 1984, p. 628, note 10.

[3]Kent Masterson-Brown, "Lee at Gettysburg: The Man, the Myth, the Recriminations," *Virginia County's Civil War,* vol. I, Middleburg, Va., Country Publishers, 1983, p. 35.

[4]Harry W. Pfanz, *Gettysburg: The Second Day,* Chapel Hill, University of North Carolina Press, 1988, p. 4.

tive. We cannot know for sure. Such questions show some of the frustrations of inference; at times we cannot know whether the answers we give to questions are right or wrong; we can know only what seems plausible or believable.

We can infer some qualities about General Lee. He shows here a delightful sense of humor, an appreciation of people around him, and seemingly a concern that his wife not worry about him. Did he really forget the name of the disease that the doctors supposed he might have, or was he seeking to minimize the entire experience to keep his wife from worrying about him? It is difficult to know, but we may infer throughout the letter a wish to put his wife's mind at ease.

Examples of inference abound in the writing of history about any subject. The French medievalist Jacques Le Goff has classified the standing of various jobs in the Middle Ages by noting those jobs that the church refused to allow priests to hold. If a priest could not hold the job, LaGoff reasoned, it must be work generally scorned. He mentioned the jobs of innkeepers, owners of bathhouses, and jugglers, among others.

Many scholars have used wills as points of inference. Wills bequeathing possessions obviously show what the maker of the will possessed, and that information may in turn show some things about the life that person lived, but wills can show other things as well. In England, for example, we may get some indication of the degree of orthodox Catholic sentiment in the sixteenth century by looking at the religious formulae expressed in wills. If we have formulae mentioning the Virgin Mary and the saints, we may infer strong Catholic sentiment. If we have formulae that mention only God and Christ, we may have some form of Protestantism.

The laws of any society provide a rich field for inference. Laws do not come out of thin air; they reflect the values of the people who make them, and they respond to conduct that usually runs counter to those values. Laws are not made by just anybody but by the people who have economic, religious, or military power in the society and who can then enforce their values on the rest. We can infer the nature of that power by looking at these laws, and we can also see the conduct that rulers assume runs against those values.

When you make an inference important to your study of the sources, you become a questioner. You do not read your sources passively; you read them actively, trying to fill in the gaps that you always find in them.

STATISTICS

Statistical information has become a major source for writing history. Modern governments keep statistics with religious passion. The United States Census, taken every ten years, offers a wealth of information, and the Bureau of the Census in Washington is a temple of numbers. Other agencies, public and private, collect statistics with the same avid compulsion. And as the *Annales* historians have shown, records in the past can be converted into statistical information by means of the assiduous use of the computer.

Statistics require interpretation. By themselves, they tell us little; what we infer from them may tell us a great deal, but if we infer wrongly, we can make some serious errors. To some students of history, the study of statistics seems tedious; to others it is exciting and original, a new window into the past. The statistical interest of historians has come about partly because statistics are available, partly because computers have made using statistics much easier, and partly because of a change in philosophy among historians themselves.

The change in philosophy is that many historians no longer believe that the most important subjects of history are the great leaders, the heroes, the villains, the writers and speakers, the famous and the notorious. These historians have become much more interested in the common people, the masses who have left us few direct records and whose names and personalities have often been lost to history.

These masses have not vanished without a trace. By applying statistical reasoning to such records as we have, we can sometimes understand who these people were, what they were thinking, what questions most agitated them, how they lived, and how they received some of the new ideas of their times. What influences prepared the way for the Protestant Reformation of the sixteenth century? Statistical information offers some clues. We have a fairly good idea what books were most popular among literate people in sixteenth- and seventeenth-century England by seeing what sorts of titles were the most frequently published. (The titles of all surviving English books published in that time have been catalogued.) We can study at second hand the emotions of the people by looking at the kinds of illustrations popular pamphleteers thought were most appealing or exciting, and these can be classified and counted. For more recent times, we can often infer what people were reading by counting such things as the number of copies sold of a book or the number of books about a certain subject.

We infer, for example, that a great many English readers wanted to read stories about saints in early sixteenth-century England, because in modern catalogues listing the titles of books published in that period, titles involving the saints turn up with great frequency. A few years later—even in countries that remained Catholic—books about saints declined in proportion to books about other subjects.

The near-worship of statistics by modern bureaucratic societies makes the task of the historian both easier and harder as we move from the Renaissance to the present. The task is more easy because statistical information nowadays is recorded in precise, accessible, and usable forms. We can know, for example, the predominant ethnic and economic composition of various voting precincts in the United States, and we can know how those precincts voted in various elections. We can analyze the difference in voting patterns between, say, an Italian Catholic precinct and a conservative Jewish precinct in a large American city such as New York or Boston. We may then infer what issues accounted for the differences or similarities we may discover. Analysis of the voting patterns of such precincts—an analysis made familiar by the media—helps us understand why one candidate won and the other lost or why one may win and why the other may lose.

The use of statistics to understand voting patterns only scratches the surface of the possible uses of statistical information by historians. The data gathered by the United States Bureau of the Census and by a myriad of government agencies allow us to infer many things about populations—whether they go to church or not, whether they practice birth control, whether they send their children to school, whether they go to college, how many times they move, how much family income they have, and so on and so on.

Private polls by agencies such as the Gallup organization, the Nielsen Ratings company, and many others tell us about changes in taste: What television programs were most popular in the 1950s? How did public opinion develop with regard to United States entry into World War II? When did George Bush begin to lose his popularity? When did the American people begin to lose confidence in American-made automobiles, and when did their confidence in such products return? Such information can be found in the reference room of almost any large library.

The use of statistical information is possible whenever we can reduce evidence to numbers. Numbers measure things. But what do we measure? That is always the question. We can choose to measure some things that tell us a great deal, or others that tell us nothing significant. One of the more controversial books based on statistics in recent years has been *Time on the Cross: The Economics of American Negro Slavery* by Robert William Fogel and Stanley L. Engerman— as the title indicates, an effort to see the face of slavery by looking at statistics left over from slave days before the American Civil War. In reviewing the book, historian Oscar Handlin discussed the contention of the authors that the average age of slave mothers when they gave birth to their first child was 22.5 years. Handlin pointed out that Fogel and Engerlman drew their data from wills probated in "fifty-four counties in eight Southern States between 1775 and 1865 which enumerated 80,000 slaves."[5]

Eighty thousand is a considerable figure. One might assume that statistical data drawn from such a sampling would have validity. But what about the significance the authors put on their finding that the average age of slave mothers was 22.5 years? The authors argued that slave mothers were mature women at the birth of their first child and that therefore they must have been married. This fairly late age for the first birth would indicate a stable family life. Yet that is not clear, though Fogel and Engerman used this evidence to infer that sexual promiscuity among slaves was limited and that family life was close and enduring. Handlin argues that such an elaborate conclusion cannot be drawn from this evidence.[6]

Handlin's thoughts about the work of Fogel and Engerman are worth pondering, for difficulties abound in using statistics. Sometimes the quantity of statistical information available may seem daunting. Anyone is likely to feel overwhelmed by a project that may involve seemingly endless tables of numbers, charts, and graphs. The interpretation of statistics requires a high level of skill. Statistics is a substantial academic discipline in itself, involving a rigorous introduction to the methods of interpreting statistics to make sense. Even with such instruction, errors in interpretation are common. Numbers may provide a comforting appearance of exactitude to some students, but the appearance may not match the reality.

---

[5]Oscar Handlin, *Truth in History*, Cambridge, Harvard University Press, 1981, p. 211.

[6]Handlin, pp. 210–226. This is only part of the lengthy criticism Handlin directs against the use of statistics in *Time on the Cross*.

Statistics cannot measure the intensity of beliefs. In political campaigns, polls show what percentage of a sampling of voters favors this or that candidate. But do those supporters feel strongly enough about their favorites to vote for them? The candidate who can get out his or her supporters may have a great advantage over the candidate who may be supported in a lukewarm way by a much larger number of citizens. Various polls throughout the 1960s showed that a majority of Americans supported the Vietnam War. But it seems now that the minority that opposed the war held its convictions with much more intensity and seemed willing to risk much more for them.

Some questions go beyond the power of statistics to measure. Many critics of the quantitative method of writing history protest that its practitioners often claim to know more about the past than they really do. Nothing takes the place, say the critics, of understanding history through the lively written words of those who participated in it; to these more humanistically inclined historians, statistics are skeletons without muscle and breath. The quantitative historians reply that the humanistic historians go on and on arguing over the same old things and that if statistics are often inexact, they are nonetheless more reliable than the impressionistic work of thinkers who are historians writing about other thinkers who made history.

No doubt, the use of statistics helps us go where other sources will not allow us entry. How far they allow us to go remains debatable, and the debate will continue. The quantitative historians will continue to flourish just because the multitude of records will draw interest, and computers seem to take gargantuan steps every year in their ability to process numbers.

If you do an essay based on quantitative research in one of your courses, be sure that you do have enough data and that you learn enough about interpreting statistics to avoid obvious errors. Be cautious. You may, for example, examine the voting records precinct by precinct for the two referendums the State of Tennessee took on secession from the Union in 1861. The first referendum, taken before the firing on Fort Sumter, showed a clear majority for staying in the Union. The second showed a majority for secession, and Tennessee duly joined the Confederacy—the last of the Confederate states to do so. In both referendums, the upper counties of East Tennessee voted solidly to remain in the Union. Having looked at those statistics, you would be most unwise to conclude that the vote for the Union was a vote for enlightened treatment of blacks as equal to whites in the

South. Other statistics would show that relative to the rest of the South, Tennessee had fewer slaves, and the issue of slavery was not so important economically as it was in the so-called cotton belt. Therefore Tennesseans saw little value in a secession movement intended to protect slavery. East Tennessee was one of the few industrial areas in the South, and its rail connections and markets were with the Northeast.

Yet during the war Tennessean Nathan Bedford Forrest, a Confederate cavalry officer, ordered that black Union soldiers captured at Fort Pillow be massacred. And shortly after the war, the Ku Klux Klan was begun in Pulaski, Tennessee. One of the Klan's major aims was to keep blacks from voting. So there is much evidence to show that the opposition to secession on the part of many Tennesseans had little to do with humanitarian concern for black Americans.

Never try to claim too much for any methodology we use in the study of history. Statistics can be a tool to unlock historical puzzles—but only if the historian knows the limits of statistical analysis and operates within those limits. Polls regularly ask a sampling of Americans to name the people they admire most. The President of the United States is also always high on the list, as are various actors, athletes, and the occasional well-known religious figure, including the Pope and sometimes this or that Protestant evangelist. But a historian would be foolish indeed to suppose that the results of such a poll measured much more than what the respondents think they should respond when a stranger asks them such a question. The woman who says that she admires a selfless minister of religion more than anybody else on earth might in secret admire the man who won $25 million in the lottery and spent all the money on the biggest party in the history of the world.

Skepticism is one of the historian's finest qualities. Throughout all historical inquiries, the relentless application of the journalistic questions will make you an active researcher and a historian of authority. Nothing is quite as destructive to a historian's reputation as to present conclusions that prove gullibility, laziness, or the simple inability to ask questions that make the data provide real insight into the meaning of the past.

3

Modes of Historical Writing

Like other writers, historians use the four common modes of expression—description, narration, exposition, and argument. We may use all the modes in a single paper. A narrative paragraph may tell how British troops ferried across the Back Bay of Boston on the night of April 18, 1775, and were required to stand in a marsh in water up to their knees waiting for supplies they did not need before they marched out to Lexington and Concord. A descriptive paragraph might give details of the marsh and the chill of the "little ice age" that made the New England spring extremely cold in that period, and a brief exposition might consider the effects on tempers of having to march 12 or 15 miles to Lexington in cold, wet clothes and wet shoes. A writer might then argue that the needless delay in the Cambridge marsh robbed the British of the element of surprise and led to their humiliating defeat at the hands of the American minutemen in the battles that began the Revolutionary War.

Although the four modes often overlap, they are distinct, and one will usually predominate in a given book or essay. If you have a clear idea of the mode best suited to your purposes in an essay, you make the task easier for you and your readers.

DESCRIPTION

Description presents an account of sensory experience—the way things look, feel, taste, sound, and smell. Popular history includes vivid descriptions, and you can describe people and places with great effect in a paper intended for a college or scholarly audience. No matter how learned or unlearned we are in the limitless facts of a historical period, we have all had sensory experiences similar to those of people in the past. Our senses are the fundamental common denominator of human life. Perhaps as a consequence of our own reliance on sense experience, we like concrete details about physical reality in books and articles about history. Details reassure us that the world of the past was enough like our own world to let us imagine it, to place ourselves within it for at least a moment, and to find it familiar and at least partly understandable.

You can tell how a building or a landscape looks. You can describe the condition of people in a sculpture, a photograph, or a painting—how they dressed, their facial expressions, and whether they were tired, happy, wet, dry, miserable, in anguish, or whatever. Even if you include a photograph, a drawing, or a painting in your essay or book, your description of it may help readers see things in it they might otherwise miss. You may describe the appearance of an object—a tool, weapon, piece of furniture, landscape, building, or portrait. You can describe geography—the mountains of Greece, the situation of a battlefield, the rivers of Africa. You can write about how the wind sounded on the American Plains as innumerable pioneers (keeping innumerable journals) went overland toward their new homes.

You can tell, as Barbara Tuchman does in her book *The Guns of August,* how troops in World War I stank so that the towns they occupied reeked with the stench of sweat-soaked clothing. You can write of the heat of summers in Washington, D.C., when Franklin Roosevelt was building his New Deal in a world before air conditioning but when public figures were expected to conduct business in wool suits and carefully knotted neckties; you can tell how the food of the American slave tasted in the years before the Civil War.

Few historical papers are devoted to description alone—though an account of the geography of the Battle of Thermopylae might be largely devoted to a description of the Malliac Gulf and the narrow ledge or pass between it and Mount Callidromion. There, in August of 480 B.C., three hundred Spartans stood off thousands of Persians until the Spartans died to the last man. Since then the hot sulphur springs of Thermopylae (the word means "hot gates" in Greek) have continued to flow, perhaps contributing to the silting up of the gulf, which has made the sea recede. On the site it is difficult to work out the exact geography of the battle. A paper on the battle might be carefully descriptive, providing the writer's reconstruction of those events and the geography that controlled them.

Never try to describe everything. You will suffocate your essay in details. Describe only enough to kindle the imaginations of readers.

In his book *Sacco and Vanzetti: The Case Resolved,* part history and part autobiography, Francis Russell tells us how he changed his mind about the celebrated trial in 1921 and execution in 1927 of Nicola Sacco and Bartolemeo Vanzetti. The two were accused of murder in a payroll robbery that took place in South Braintree, Massachusetts, on April 15, 1920. They were tried in Dedham, Massachusetts. More than thirty years ago Russell began his interest in the case by believing that they were innocent. After long and detailed study, he concluded that Sacco was guilty of murder and that Vanzetti was what in legal terminology is called an accessory after the fact.

The following descriptive passage sets the tone for the carefully reflective book that follows:

Someday, I promised myself, I was going to sit down and study the Sacco-Vanzetti trial transcript. But with the coming of the war, my interest lapsed. If I had not been called for a month's jury duty in the Dedham courthouse in the spring of 1953, I doubt that I should ever have concerned myself with the case again. I was then living in Wellesley, eight miles away, and when the weather was good I used to walk along the back roads to Dedham. By starting at quarter to eight I could get to the courthouse just before ten o'clock, when the morning session began. I liked those brisk bright mornings, the earth smelling of spring, the maples in misty shades of mauve and red. From Wellesley the road dipped past the country club, curving down to Needham, a semi-suburb of repetitive three-bedroom houses, commonplace enough, yet—as I was later to discover—singularly interwoven with the Sacco-Vanzetti case. Spring was late that year. Not until my second week, as I crossed the bridge over the Charles River the other side of Needham, did I hear the creaky notes of the redwings among last year's cattails. A few mornings later I saw a couple of painted turtles still torpid from hibernation. From the bridge I headed up the winding road to Dedham, past much empty land, orchards, stone walls, and the driveways of discreetly hidden river estates. Then, from Common Street on Dedham's outskirts, I swung into High Street, ahead of me above the still-bare elms the courthouse dome, mosquelike in the early light, crowned by an ornate metal grille and a flagpole. On those placid mornings the flag hung limp. It was almost a third of a century since Sacco and Vanzetti had been tried, yet the ghost of their trial still seemed to haunt the courthouse. Scarcely a day passed while I was on jury duty but some reference to it came up. It shadowed us all. We served in the same paneled room with the marble-faced clock where Sacco and Vanzetti had been tried and sentenced. There was the same enclosure for the prisoners that Sacco-Vanzetti partisans referred to as a "cage"—as if the two defendants had been exhibited like animals in a zoo. Actually, it was a waist-high metal lattice, slightly higher in the back, with nothing formidable or forbidding about it. Our white-haired sheriff, Samuel Capen, in his blue-serge cutaway, its gleaming brass buttons embossed with the state seal, and his white staff of office that he wielded like a benevolent shepherd, had been sheriff at the time of the great trial. In the overlong lunch hours he would sometimes talk about it, telling of the day Sacco and Vanzetti were sentenced, how Vanzetti made his famous speech, and how Judge Thayer sat with his head bent and never looked at him. I don't suppose any doubts had ever crossed the sheriff's mind as to the guilt of the two Italians or the rectitude of Massachusetts justice.[1]

We have several forms of description here. We have a direct appeal to the senses as when Russell tells us of colors ("misty shades of mauve and red"), objects ("the marble-faced clock") sounds ("the creaky notes of the redwings") and smells ("the earth smelling of spring").

All these descriptions of physical reality depend on our already having had some experience with them. When he tells us that the Dedham courthouse dome looked "mosquelike in the early light," he assumes that we have at least seen pictures of mosques so that we can get a rough idea of what he saw. We may not have had every experience he describes; for example some readers may not have heard "the creaky notes" of redwing blackbirds. Still these readers follow Russell's account because his description conveys authority: he has been there; he knows what he is talking about; his language conveys a familiar reality. These qualities help readers believe the writer.

Another kind of description here is more impressionistic. He tells us that the enclosure where prisoners sat in the courtroom had "nothing formidable or forbidding about it." He tells us that the sheriff carried an official staff "that he wielded like a benevolent shepherd." These are the writer's impressions. Someone else might have seen the "waist-high metal lattice, slightly higher in the back" as formidable and forbidding and might have judged that Sheriff Capen wielded his official staff like a warrior's club. Subtly, Russell has prepared us to believe his impressions because he has provided earlier vivid and believable details about his observations. He has created an "implied au-

[1]Francis Russell, *Sacco and Vanzetti: The Case Resolved,* New York, Harper & Row, 1986, 34–36.

thor"—dispassionate, warm-hearted, and sharply observant, a writer we can trust. So we believe him readily when he passes to more subjective, impressionistic observations—the unthreatening quality of the prisoner's "cage," the benevolence of the sheriff's flourishing his staff of office. Description often combines these two elements—the concrete and the impressionistic.

Never make things up when you describe something. Base your descriptions on evidence. Although some readers may be entertained by flights of fancy, serious historians find them cheap and dishonest. Here are two paragraphs written by Paul Murray Kendall in his biography of Richard III, King of England between 1483 and 1485. They describe the battle of Barnet, in which Richard, then Duke of Gloucester, fought on the side of his older brother, Edward IV, against an effort by the Earl of Warwick to overthrow Edward.

> Suddenly, there was a swirl in the mist to the left of and behind the enemy's position. A shiver ran down the Lancastrian line. Exeter's men began to give way, stubbornly at first, then faster. Warwick's center must be crumbling. Richard signaled his trumpeters. The call to advance banners rang out. The weary young commander and his weary men surged forward. The hedge of steel before them began to fall apart. Then the enemy were in full flight, casting away their weapons as they ran. Out of the mist loomed the great sun banner of the House of York. A giant figure strode forward. Pushing his visor up, Richard saw that the King was smiling at him in brotherly pride. The right wing, driving westward across the Lancastrian rear, had linked up with Edward's center to bring the battle to an end. It was seven o'clock in the morning; the struggle had lasted almost three hours.[2]

Kendall's description evokes a vivid image of battle, one perhaps true in spirit to events. But his scene is almost entirely made up. Our sources for the battle of Barnet are skimpy, lacking entirely the descriptive details that Kendall gives us. Historian Charles Ross, in remarking on Kendall's account of Barnet, comments drily, "The incautious reader might be forgiven for thinking that the author himself was present at the battle."[3]

[2]Paul Murray Kendall, *Richard the Third,* New York, Doubleday, 1965, p. 97.

[3]Charles Rose, *Richard III,* Berkeley and Los Angeles, University of California Press, 1983, p. 21.

Kendall's book illustrates some of the most difficult problems of "popular" history. He writes well, and thousands of people have read his work. But his incautious exaggeration ruined his credit among historians who take seriously the limitations of their sources. Don't sacrifice accuracy in the name of vividness, or you may sacrifice your plausibility, too.

British historian John Keegan is much more circumspect in his description of the physical circumstances of the Battle of Waterloo in 1815, where the British and the Prussians defeated Napoleon once and for all. Keegan knows some things from his sources and infers cautiously from them, using the word "probably" to let you know that he is conjecturing.

> Besides being hungry and travel-worn the combatants at Waterloo were clearly rain-sodden. The regiments that had spent the night marching lay down to sleep in wet clothes and probably woke up to fight the battle still very damp. Those which passed the night in the fields, though they slept worse, or had no sleep at all, generally found means to dry out after sunrise. A young officer of the 32nd, who had woken wet through, managed to get into a shed where there was a fire, and the men made large fires outside. The light company men of the 3rd Foot Guards, who had spent the night "cramped sitting on the side of a wet ditch" south of Hougoumont, got a fire going "which served to dry our clothing and accoutrements," and Leeke, of the 52nd, found a fire large and hot enough to get some sleep by. Wood, of the 10th Hussars, an officer whose Waterloo letter breathes the authentic cavalry spirit, "got into a small cottage close to our bivouac . . . most of us naked, and getting our things dry at the fire. . . . Old Quentin burned his boots and could not get them on." Other cavalrymen, too, found their clothes spoiled by the wet. The Greys' scarlet jackets had run into their white belts overnight, and Sergeant Coglan of the 18th Hussars attempted to dry his clothes by hanging them on the branches of trees. The Assembly was sounded before he had succeeded, and he dressed in the saddle, "crying out to those I had charge of to mount also." Waterloo day was overcast, rather than sunny, so those who, like Coglan, failed to get near a fire at the beginning presumably stayed damp until well after midday. Houssaye's "kaleidoscope of vivid hues and metallic flashes," his "bright green jackets, . . . imperial blue collars, . . . white breeches, . . . breastplates of gold, . . . blue coats faced with scarlet, . . . red kurkas and blue plastrons, . . . green dolmans embroi-

dered with yellow braid, [and] red pelisses edged with fur" must have covered many limp stocks, sticky shirts, and clammy socks.[4]

We can see here the common denominator of sense experience. We know what it is to have to go about in wet clothes, we recognize colors, and we know how hard it is to dry things in the open on an overcast day—or at least we know enough about wetness and overcast days to imagine that we know these things. I can imagine a soldier pulling wet clothes onto his body in great haste because I have sometimes had to put on wet clothes, and I recall the miserable experience.

Keegan shows that description can give not only a sense of immediacy but can make us understand the events better. His intended thesis throughout the book is to answer this question: "How do men act in battle?" His description of the men's condition in the British and the French armies on the day of Waterloo as it fits into the rest of his book helps us understand his thesis.

NARRATIVE

Narratives tell stories, and narratives are the bedrock of history. Without narratives, history would die as a discipline. Narratives tell us what happened. What happened when your college was founded? What happened when the United States recognized the State of Israel in 1948? What happened during the Boston Police Strike of 1919? What happened when Woodrow Wilson imposed racial segregation in the federal civil service?

Narrative history often looks easy to write because it is relatively easy to read. In fact storytelling is a complicated art. As in description, part of the art lies in a sense of what to include and what to exclude, what to believe and what to reject. Narrative must also take into account contradictions in the evidence and either resolve them or admit frankly that they cannot be resolved. Who fired the first shot on the morning of April 19, 1775, when British regular soldiers clashed with the minutemen on the Lexington Green in Massachusetts? The incident makes a nice subject for narrative history—but it is not an easy narrative to write. Sylvanus Wood, one of the minutemen, dictated his account of the battle over fifty years afterwards. Here is part of what he said:

[4]John Keegan, *The Face of Battle*, New York, Penguin, 1984, p. 137.

Parker led those of us who were equipped to the north end of Lexington Common, near the Bedford Road, and formed us in single file. I was stationed about in the centre of the company. While we were standing, I left my place and went from one end of the company to the other and counted every man who was paraded, and the whole number was thirty-eight, and no more. . . .

The British troops approached us rapidly in platoons with a general officer on horseback at their head. The officer came up to within about two rods of the centre of the company, where I stood, the first platoon being about three rods distant. They were halted. The officer then swung his sword, and said, "Lay down your arms, you damned rebels, or you are all dead men. Fire!" Some guns were fired by the British at us from the first platoon, but no person was killed or hurt, being probably charged only with powder.

Just at this time, Captain Parker ordered every man to take care of himself. The company immediately dispersed; and while the company was dispersing and leaping over the wall, the second platoon of the British fired and killed some of our men. There was not a gun fired by any of Captain Parker's company, within my knowledge.[5]

Lieutenant John Barker of the British Army was also at Lexington, fighting with the regiment called the King's Own. He wrote an account of the battle only a few days afterwards, and here is part of what he said.

About 5 miles on this side of a town called Lexington, which lay in our road, we heard there were some hundreds of people collected together intending to oppose us and stop our going on. At 5 o'clock we arrived there and saw a number of people, I believe between 2 and 300, formed in a common in the middle of the town. We still continued advancing, keeping prepared against an attack tho' without intending to attack them; but on our coming near them they fired one or two shots, upon which our men without any orders rushed in upon them, fired and put 'em to flight. Several of them were killed, we could not tell how many because they were got behind walls and into the woods. We had a man of the 10th Light Infantry wounded, nobody else hurt.[6]

How many American minutemen waited for the British on the green at Lexington that morning? Who is the more reliable source?

[5]*The Spirit of Seventy-Six,* edited by Henry Steele Commager and Richard B. Morris, New York, Harper & Row, 1975, pp. 82–83.

[6]*The Spirit of Seventy-Six,* pp. 70–71.

Perhaps we can never know. The writer of a historical narrative must deal with the contradiction. You cannot pretend the contradiction does not exist. Often you must use some analysis in your text, some thinking about the text that will allow you to make sense of it. Here is an acceptable version of the story that remains true to the sources.

> Exactly what happened at Lexington is buried in the confusions of the morning. Sylvanus Wood, one of the Patriot soldiers, claimed that Parker threw a thin line of armed minutemen across the green to face the British regulars marching down what is now Massachusetts Avenue. Wood claims he counted the minutemen and that they numbered only thirty-eight, but Wood set down his account fifty years after the event, and his memory may have played tricks on him. British Lieutenant John Barker, marching with the King's Own regiment, said there were two or three hundred, but he may have been counting curious spectators who turned out to see the show. It was early in the morning, and Barker was angry and perhaps frightened—not emotions that might have made him count objectively. In any case the minutemen were heavily outnumbered, and Parker knew it. He ordered his men to fall back. Someone fired a shot. Barker said the shot came from the minutemen; Wood said the British fired first. We can never know who did fire the first shot, and in the confusion the British and the Patriots on the scene probably did not know either. Shooting did break out. Several minutemen were killed. The fighting of the American Revolution had begun.

Sometimes you may write the best narrative you can put together and mention the contradictions in your footnotes, perhaps explaining why you have rejected some sources and accepted others. However you do it, you must let readers know that important contradictions exist if you find them in your sources.

Narratives usually follow chronological order. You start at the beginning of the events, and you write on to the end, telling about the first events first and the last last. Sometimes good storytellers and good historians begin with some important event and then go back to explain why it happened or why it was significant. James MacGregor Burns begins the second volume of his three-volume narrative history of the United States with the following story:

> Belching clouds of steam and hazy blue smoke, the stubby little locomotive chugged along the iron rails that wove through the low allegheny [sic] Mountains. While the fireman heaved chunks of walnut and cherry into the roaring firebox, the engineer looked out

through his narrow window past the small boiler, the polished brass fittings, the stovepipe-shaped smokestack, watching for the village stations along the way: Relay House, Lutherville, Timonium. . . . In a rear coach sat Abraham Lincoln, regaling cronies with droll stories and listening imperturbably to politicians who climbed aboard to exhort and complain, while a little party of diplomats silently watched this loose-framed man who, with his seamed face, deep-sunk eyes, and rough cut of a beard, appeared in mourning even as he told his small-town anecdotes.[7]

Burns is about to tell the story of Abraham Lincoln's delivery of the Gettysburg Address at the dedication of the Gettysburg National Cemetery on November 19, 1863, four months after the great battle that had turned back Robert E. Lee's invasion of the north. It is worth saying that Burns had done thorough research on all these details—that he knew the kind of locomotive that pulled Lincoln's train and even the kind of wood locomotives burned in that part of America and the color of the smoke that cherry and walnut give off in combustion. In an endnote he gives us the evidence for each of these details; he does not make things up, as Paul Murray Kendall did. After the story of the dedication of the cemetery at Gettysburg, he goes back to tell briefly the story of the American Civil War and its significance to American history. In the book itself he develops themes introduced in this early chapter.

A good narrative begins by establishing some sort of tension, some kind of problem, that the later development of the narrative should resolve. The beginning arouses our curiosity. In the story that James MacGregor Burns tells, we ask, "Why did Lincoln go to Gettysburg?" As Burns gets into his story, we ask, "What did the Gettysburg Address signify and what did the Civil War mean to the history of the United States immediately afterwards?"

You cannot proceed far into a narrative without showing your readers that you are establishing a tension that must be resolved. You cannot hold readers' attention merely by telling them one interesting detail after another. Don't leave them wondering, "What's the point of all this?" If you do, you lose them.

Let us return to some thoughts about the nature of history sketched in the introduction to this book. Children's stories demon-

---

[7]James MacGregor Burns, *The Workshop of Democracy*, New York, Knopf, 1985, p. 3.

strate the qualities of any good narrative. We read, "Once upon a time a little girl named Cinderella lived in a house with her wicked step-mother and her two wicked stepsisters. Now the prince of the country gave a great ball, and he invited Cinderella's sisters, but poor Cinderella had to stay home and sweep out the ashes while her sisters went off and had a good time." We immediately know that Cinderella has some troubles and that somehow the story is going to involve the sisters, the step-mother, the prince, and the ball. The story will tell us why all these details are introduced at the beginning.

A good narrative in history has the same qualities. It is not merely a recitation of facts. It introduces elements in tension and the rest of the story will be about that tension. Don't introduce material into your essay at the beginning if you do not intend to do something with that material later on.

A narrative should have a climax that embodies the meaning the writer wants readers to take from the story. At the climax, everything comes together—the bill is passed, the battle is won or lost, the candidate is elected, the leader is assassinated, the speech is made, the problem is solved or else explained. Because it gathers up all the threads and joins them to make the writer's point, the climax comes near the end of the paper. When you arrive at the climax, you are ready to wrap up your story, and your readers should feel that you have kept a promise made to them in the beginning. If you cannot think of a climax to your paper, you should reexamine your topic. A good narrative has a place where everything the writer has been set-ting down comes to a head. If you cannot find a climatic point, you need to reorganize your story.

A historian of the battles of Lexington and Concord might choose to make the climax the moment at Lexington when the first shots were exchanged between the Patriots and the British. The signifi-cance of that moment would be that it marked the beginning of com-bat in the Revolutionary War. Or one might make the climax the hot skirmish that took place by the wooden bridge outside Concord later on in the day. The significance here would be that this fight forced the British to retreat, giving to the Patriots the anticipation of victory and to the British the anticipation of defeat. Or the climax might become the bloody retreat back into Boston by the British troops, under fire from every stone wall and every woods as they fell back. The signifi-cance might be the human drama of men who had walked about 45 miles, encountered opposition greater than they dreamed possible, and barely escaped with their lives while others of their number were killed.

How you end a narrative depends on what you deem significant in the story you are telling. Your climax should operate as an organizing principle for your entire paper. Your readers should realize when they get to the climax that this has been your goal all along, that they have read all these other things to get here.

Let us review some of the things we have said about narrative, now reaching back for the journalistic questions. In writing a narrative you must answer these questions. You don't have to write them down, though sometimes writing helps you think about them better. At least ponder them and be sure you have some answers.

1. Why am I telling this story?
2. Where do I want to begin?
3. What happened?
4. When did it happen?
5. Who or what caused those things to happen?
6. What were the most important events that happened and what were the less important?
7. Who were the major characters in the drama?
8. What is the climax of the story, the place where everything in the story comes to a head and where both my readers and I realize that the story is now ready to end?
9. Where do I want to end?
10. What does the story mean?
11. What details help me tell the story more effectively?
12. What details, though interesting, get in the way of my story and slow my readers down, perhaps hiding from those readers the real story I want to tell?

EXPOSITION

Expositions explain—philosophical ideas, causes of events, the significance of actions, the motives of participants, the working of an organization, the ideology of a political party. Any time you set out to explain cause and effect or the meaning of an event or an idea, you are writing in the expository mode.

As I have pointed out earlier in this chapter, exposition may coexist in an essay with other modes. The narrator who tells *what* happened usually devotes some paragraphs to telling *why* it happened— and so goes into expository writing. Some historical essays are fairly evenly balanced between narrative and exposition, telling both what happened and why, or else explaining the significance of the story. Many historical essays are primarily expositions, though one can hardly explain without making some reference to what happened that needs explanation.

You may, for example, write an essay to answer this question: What did the founding fathers mean by Second Amendment to the U.S. Constitution? That amendment reads, "A well-regulated militia, being necessary to the security of a free State, the right of the people to keep and bear arms, shall not be infringed." The essay you would write in response would be an exposition. But it might contain some narratives—the situation in 1789 when the Constitution was ratified, the situation today, the decisions of courts in the past on cases brought under the Second Amendment.

The study of the influence of one thinker on another or of one set of ideas on a historical process can make a good expository paper. You may even expound the significance of some technological invention. Here are a few expository subjects that may be appropriate in various history courses:

The view of human nature expressed in the *Federalist Papers*

A comparison between Thomas More's *Utopia* and Nicolo Machiavelli's *The Prince*

Luther's understanding of justification by faith alone

The meaning of Woodrow Wilson's attitude toward blacks

The concept of chivalry in nineteenth-century Southern literature in the United States

The influence of Sir Walter Scott's novels in the American South during the nineteenth century

All these subjects require analysis of texts, of events, or both. You must explain things, relate some things to other things, infer things, and perhaps ask some questions that no one can answer.

Here is an excerpt from one of the most famous books of the Renaissance, Baldesar Castiglione's *Book of the Courtier:*

> There are also other exercises which, although not immediately dependent upon arms, still have much in common therewith and de- mand much manly vigor; and chief among these is the hunt, it seems

to me, because it has a certain resemblance to war. It is a true pastime for great lords, it befits a Courtier, and one understands why it was so much practiced among the ancients. He should also know how to swim, jump, run, throw stones; for, besides their usefulness in war, it is frequently necessary to show one's prowess in such things, whereby a good name is to be won, especially with the crowd (with whom one must reckon after all). Another noble exercise and most suitable for a man at court is the game of tennis which shows off the disposition of body, the quickness and litheness of every member, and all the qualities that are brought out by almost every other exercise. Nor do I deem vaulting on horseback to be less worthy, which, though it is tiring and difficult, serves more than anything else to make a man agile and dextrous; and besides its usefulness, if such agility is accompanied by grace, in my opinion it makes a finer show than any other. If, then, our Courtier is more than fairly expert in such exercises, I think he ought to put aside all others, such as vaulting on the ground, rope-walking, and the like, which smack of the juggler's trade and little befit a gentleman.[8]

Here is an exposition that uses this passage as part of a general treatment of the Renaissance. Insofar as possible, the expositor puts the thoughts of Castiglione in other words, words that may be more familiar and hence more understandable for readers today.

Baldesar Castiglione's Book of the Courtier, the most frequently translated and printed book of the sixteenth century other than the Bible, presents itself as a dialogue on the qualities that make a good courtier. Courtiers, as the name implies, were members of a prince's court or entourage, helping him in various ways to rule his domain. In the sixteenth century, when Italy was divided among multitudes of city-states, princes needed talented men to help conduct finances, war, diplomacy, and other affairs so they might retain power over a fickle and often rebellious populace. Courtiers rose on their talents but also on their ability to get along with other people and to impress their

[8]Baldassare Castiglione, *The Book of the Courtier,* trans. Charles S. Singleton, Garden City, NY, Doubleday, 1959, pp. 38–39.

princes. Castiglione's dialogue became not only an en-
tertainment but also a sort of handbook. Aspiring
courtiers read it to learn how to conduct themselves as
gentlemen and how to rise. It was the great manners
book of its day, popular alike with Spanish kings and
English puritans. Castiglione throughout writes on two
levels. On one level the courtiers in his dialogue discuss ways of becoming more useful, better men. It is good
to hunt, for example, for hunting calls for many of the
same skills required in war. Evidently he referred to
life in the open air, to riding on horseback in the
chase, and to marksmanship--all helpful training for
soldiers. Swimming, jumping, running, and throwing
stones offer what we would call physical conditioning
and provide a sort of basic training for war.

On another level Castiglione's characters are always
concerned not only to better their skills but also to
make a good impression. By performing feats of physical
strength and agility, one wins a good name with the
crowd "with whom one must reckon after all." Tennis
with its leaping and quickness displays the body.
Jumping on horseback both helps a man become "agile and
dextrous" and "makes a finer show than any other." Some
things make a bad show and are to be avoided no matter
how useful they might be as bodily exercises. For some
reason Castiglione cites "vaulting on the ground" as an
act to be avoided, perhaps because that sort of leaping
was a game of peasants who could not afford jumping
horses. "Rope-walking," balancing oneself on a tight
rope, is also scorned because it is one of the tricks
of "jugglers," the traveling entertainers who put on
shows for city crowds much as their spiritual descen-
dants do today. Such entertainers were considered lower
class and even slightly dishonorable. They were often
magicians and practiced sleight of hand, and their use

of trickery smacked of deceit. The laws of the church
forbade priests to be "jugglers," and Castiglione obviously felt that would-be courtiers lowered themselves
by learning such skills.

Throughout his big book, these two qualities come to
the fore again and again--skill and reputation. The
good courtier in Castiglione's mind possessed both.
Thousands of readers pored over his pages to learn not
only what they should be but what they should seem to be.

This exposition tries to make sense of a text from the past. Our
world has greatly changed from Castiglione's. The exposition explains
his ideas to us and defines some terms and provides a context for his
thoughts. Castiglione used the common word *juggler,* which we might
interpret as someone who tosses several balls in the air at once without dropping any of them. The older meaning of the term in both
Castiglione's Italian and in English was a street entertainer, usually
some sort of magician. By explaining this broader use of the term, the
writer makes the text he is expounding more clear. Always define the
essential terms of your exposition.

The exposition includes some inferences. The writer infers that
juggling is forbidden to the courtier because it smacks of deceit, and
courtiers are supposed to be honest. The writer infers that jumping or
"vaulting" on the ground is forbidden because that sort of athletic ac-
tivity is common to peasants who cannot afford horses. One cannot
prove an inference, but inferences provide plausible explanations that
may help fill out the meaning of a text. These inferences show a
writer thinking and trying to make sense of things, and readers appreciate such thinking as long as it stays within the boundaries of what
seems reasonable.

ARGUMENT

Historians use argument to take a position on a controversial subject.
It can be said that every paper contains an argument in that every paper has a main theme the writer wants us to believe. Yet in common
usage, an argument is part of a debate, a dialogue between opposing
views. Arguments include exposition, for they must explain the

writer's point of view. An argumentative essay also seeks to prove that other points of view are wrong.

Arguments are most interesting when the issues are important and both sides are fair to each other. The questions that create good arguments arise naturally as historians do their research, weigh evidence, and make judgments that may not persuade others. Was Christianity, as Edward Gibbon held in the eighteenth century, a major cause for the decline and fall of the Roman Empire? Was Martin Luther hostile to Jews? Did Al Smith lose the presidential election of 1928 to Herbert Hoover because Smith was a Catholic? Was slavery the main cause of the American Civil War? Did the peace movement in the United States shorten or prolong the Vietnam War?

The writing of history abounds with arguments about what happened and why. These arguments arise because the evidence can be interpreted in opposing ways. Sometimes arguments go on until a consensus is gradually achieved. Did the German General Staff expect England to fight for Belgian neutrality if Germany invaded Belgium in 1914? For a long time many historians claimed that if England had declared itself clearly before fighting started, Germany would not have sent armies into Belgium. But since the work of German historian Fritz Fischer, most historians have come around to the view that Germany planned all along to fight the English. Sometimes arguments rage for years, die down, smolder awhile, and flame up again. Was Socrates a threat to Athenian society, as his judges claimed in his trial in when he was condemned to death? Consensus seemed to be reached that he was not, but a book by journalist I. F. Stone has raised the issue once again, and his book has been attacked by modern defenders of Socrates.

In any important issue in history, you will find disagreement among historians. These disagreements are particularly evident in book reviews. A historian who disagrees with another will make a counterargument to a book the reviewer thinks incorrect. Jacob Burckhardt's History of the Renaissance in Italy published in 1860 has provoked a virtual library of response, books and articles arguing that he was right or wrong in his interpretation of the Renaissance—or arguing that he was partly right and partly wrong. Frederick Jackson Turner's frontier thesis has been similarly provocative.

The usual experience of the student of history is to study a great deal and to become convinced that someone else's argument is wrong. Francis Russell's books on the Sacco and Vanzetti case represent this sort of discovery. The popular consensus has been that Sacco and

Vanzetti were innocent Italian immigrants hounded to their death by a vicious Yankee society for murders they did not commit. In 1955 Russell wrote an article supporting this point of view, published first in the *Antioch Review* and reprinted three years later with photographs in *American Heritage*. Slowly he changed his mind, and his publication of *Tragedy in Dedham* and *Sacco and Vanzetti: The Case Resolved* represents a formidable attack on the previous consensus.

Stay tuned to your own intellectual impulses when you read sources. Where do the arguments of others seem weak? Where do you feel uneasy about your own arguments? Can you make the evidence point to another conclusion? Often, good argument is simply a matter of common sense: Can we believe that something might have happened the way a writer tells us it happened? Many haters of President Franklin Roosevelt argued that Roosevelt knew about the Japanese attack on Pearl Harbor in 1941 before it happened but kept it secret because he wanted the United States to go to war. Such a conspiracy would have involved dozens, even hundreds of people— those who had broken the Japanese secret code for sending messages to the military and diplomats, those who monitored Japanese broadcasts, those who translated them and took the translations to the State Department and to the White House, and the officials to whom they all reported. Is it plausible that such a vast conspiracy could have taken place without anyone who was part of it ever stepping forward to talk about it? Our experience with human beings and their apparently uncontrollable yearning to tell secrets would seem to indicate that the answer to such a question would be no.

Good arguments are founded on skepticism. Come to history as a doubter. Study the evidence over and over. Read what other historians have said. See what the sources say. Listen to your own uneasiness. Don't take anything for granted. And when you decide to argue, make as careful a case as you can.

RULES FOR ARGUMENT IN HISTORICAL WRITING

Here are a few rules that will help you make convincing arguments. Study them carefully, and keep them in mind when you are reading the arguments of others.

1. Always state your own argument quickly and concisely, as early as possible in your paper.

Get to the point in the first paragraph if you can. You will help yourself in making an argument if you state your premises early. "Premises" are assumptions on which your arguments are based. In writing about history, you may assume that some sources are reliable and some are not, and you will choose to base your argument on the reliable sources. You will then have to explain why you think that one source is more reliable than another; having done that, you can then move toward your argument based on the premise of reliability.

2. When you make an assertion essential to your case, provide some examples as evidence.

Assertions alone cannot carry an argument, no matter how sincere you are about them or how true you think they may be. Readers must always have some reason to believe you.

3. Always give the fairest possible treatment to those people against whom you may be arguing.

Never distort the work of someone who disagrees with your position. Such distortions are cowardly and unfair, and if you are found out in such conduct, readers will reject your work—the good part along with the bad. Treat your adversaries as erring friends, not as foes to be slain, and you will always be more convincing to the great mass of readers who want writers to be fair and benign in argument. The most effective scholarly arguments are carried on courteously and without bitterness or anger.

4. Always admit weaknesses in your argument or acknowledge those facts that opponents might raise against your position.

If you deny obvious truths about the subject you are arguing, knowledgeable readers will see what you are doing and will lose confidence in your objectivity. If you admit the weaknesses or the counter-arguments, you will appear more authoritative and more honest, and readers will be more inclined to agree with your arguments.

Concession is a vital power in argument. You may concede that certain facts stand against your position. But you may then argue either that those facts are not as important as the facts you adduce for your argument, or that those facts have been misinterpreted. In either case you acknowledge that you know about the contrary facts, and you rob your foes of seeming to catch you in ignorance.

5. Stay on the subject throughout your essay so that your argument is not submerged in meaningless detail.

Writers may be tempted to put everything they know into a paper. They have worked hard to gather the information, they find it interesting, and they want readers to see how much work they have done and how much they know. So, they pad papers with much information not relevant to the subject at hand. Sometimes they begin with pages and pages of background information and get into their argument only after they have bewildered readers with a story that does not need to be told. If you argue that, say, Lyndon Johnson's Civil Rights Act of 1964 was a landmark in American history, you do not have to give us Johnson's biography to make your point.

6. Avoid common fallacies.

"Fallacies" are illogical arguments that pose as logical statements. You may be familiar with the term *straw man*. People set up straw men when they argue against positions that their opponents have not taken or when, without evidence, they attribute bad motives to opponents. A historian might argue that the sixteenth century was marked by much skepticism in matters of religion; an opponent might unjustly argue in response that the sixteenth century could not have experienced religious skepticism because the scientific world view of Galileo and Newton was unknown—as if religious skepticism depended on a scientific world view. Worse, opponents might argue that because the historian was not religious himself, he wanted to find skepticism in the sixteenth century. Neither of these issues has anything to do with the original argument; they set up straw men, arguments that may be easily defeated and so give the appearance of victory—except that they are beside the point.

Don't assume that merely because something happened after something else, the first happening caused the second. Various forms of this fallacy abound in historical writing. (The common Latin term often used to describe this fallacy is *post hoc ergo propter hoc,* "Because this happened after that, it happened because of that.") Some religious people have argued that because art recovered from the ruins of Pompei show vivid portrayals of homosexual and heterosexual intercourse, the Roman Empire fell on account of sexual promiscuity. Pompei was destroyed by a volcanic eruption of Mt. Vesuvius in 79 A.D. The last Roman emperor in the West was deposed in 476 A.D. It would seem a bit extreme to say that because there was sexual license in the first century, Rome fell in the sixth century. Historical causation is much more complicated than that.

A more subtle problem with this fallacy arises with events that are closely related though one does not necessarily cause the other. The stock market in New York crashed in October 1929; the Great Depression followed. The crash contributed to the lack of confidence that made the Great Depression a terrible event, but it would be a distortion to say that the crash caused the Depression. Both seem to have been caused by the same economic forces. It is in this sort of relation that it becomes most necessary to think out the various strands of causation and to avoid making things too simple.

By all means avoid the bandwagon fallacy, the easy assumption that because a great number of historians agree on a certain issue, their position must be the right one. Consensus by experts is not to be scorned, but experts can also be prone to prejudices. Francis Russell tells of the rush of hostility directed against him when he attacked the previous consensus about the Sacco-Vanzetti case. Great historical work has been done by people who went doggedly in pursuit of the evidence against the influence of the consensus. But be sure you have evidence when you attack a consensus.

Thinking about modes of writing will help you define more precisely the reason for your paper in history. Too frequently in history courses, students start writing without having any idea of why they are writing or what point they finally want to make about a topic. Forcing yourself to think about the modes will make you examine your own purposes. That examination will make your writing easier. It will also help your readers understand your purposes quickly and follow your prose as you develop your thoughts.

4

Gathering Information and Writing Drafts

Any sort of writing is hard work. Writing history has its special problems—many of them already discussed in this book. But most people can learn to do it successfully. The frustrations are immense, and every writer suffers them, but the rewards of good writing make the labor worthwhile.

To start, you may need to rid yourself of some common superstitions. One is that writers are somehow inspired, that real writers sit down at their desks and turn out articles and books with the greatest of ease. Another is that if you must write several drafts of anything, you are not a good writer. Still another is that if you labor to get on paper what you want to say, you are not going to improve it very much if you write a second or even a third draft.

A few writers manage to write without revising—but only a few. The almost unanimous testimony of good writers in all disciplines is that writing is always difficult and that they must write several drafts to be satisfied with an essay or a book. A rule of thumb holds that the easier a piece of writing is to read, the harder it was to write.

Good writers work through to a clear understanding of their own thoughts. All writers sometimes begin an essay without a clear idea of what they think or what they want to say. The process of writing and rewriting clarifies their thoughts and strengthens their hold on their own ideas. Once they have worked out an essay, they have ideas that cannot be blown away by the first person who comes along with a firm opinion. Writing has this confirming quality, valuable for all those who want to know their own minds.

All writers use some sort of process—a series of steps that lead them from discovering a subject to writing a final draft. Different writers work according to different rituals. Eventually you will find your own way of doing things. In this chapter we shall walk through some steps followed by many writers on their way to books or essays. These suggestions may help you. At least they will illuminate the way you go about writing and perhaps help you understand it better and make it more efficient.

I. FIND A TOPIC

History papers begin with an assignment:

A requirement of this course will be a research paper. Choose a topic. Let me approve it. Make it ten to fifteen pages long. Don't make it longer than fifteen pages. The paper will be due two weeks before the end of the term.

I want you to write a ten-page paper defending the British side in the dispute between Great Britain and the American colonies that led to the American Revolution.

You must do a book review for this course.

Specific assignments come with a built-in advantage: You know what you are going to write about before you start. Nowadays most assignments in history courses are probably more like the first one in this list. You are told that the paper must be on a topic related to the course and that it must be a certain length. If it is a research paper, you assume that it will involve work in the library, and you must document your sources with footnotes or endnotes and bibliography. What will you write about? That is up to you.

For many students, finding the topic is an ordeal. Professional historians have the same problem. The ability to find your own topic reflects both how much you know the material and how well you can think about it. Defining your own topics is good discipline. A liberal arts education—including education in history—should teach you to ask questions and ponder meanings in every text you encounter in life. It's good practice to do such pondering in a history course.

Start with your own interests. You must have some interest in the material, or you would not have taken the course. You must be curious about people, events, documents, or problems considered in the course. This curiosity should make you pose some questions naturally. Why did Machiavelli say that it is better to be feared than loved? Was Samuel Gompers conservative or progressive? What in the character of President Ulysses S. Grant made him a good general and a bad president? How historical is Gore Vidal's novel *Julian* or his novel *Lincoln?* Why was the novel *Gone with the Wind* so popular? How has capital punishment evolved in America?

Most people ask such questions all the time. We can answer some of them if we work hard on them. Good historians take their own questions seriously enough to try to answer them.

Sometimes you may be interested in a well-worn topic. Why did the Confederate Army under General Lee lose at Gettysburg? What qualities of Christianity made it attractive to people in the Roman Empire during the first three centuries after Christ? What was humanism in the Renaissance? Don't be afraid to tackle these problems. Yes, at first glance you may think that everything has been said that can be said. But when you look at the sources, you may discover that you have an insight that is new and different and worth exploring. The possibility is especially good if you study a few documents carefully and use them as windows to open into the age or the event that produced them.

If nothing else, you can survey the literature about these problems and write about the contradictory conclusions various historians have made from the same evidence. Such interpretative essays on the work of other historians are common and valuable, for they show the state of knowledge and debate about a historical problem that is interesting enough to attract good minds.

Here I must repeat one of my most important axioms: Yours should be an *informed* interest. You have to know something before you can write anything about history. Don't write an opinionated article off the top of your head. Good historians read, ask questions of their reading, read again, and try to get things right. It is typical of a historian to write with a pile of notes or a collection of notebooks beside the paper or the keyboard.

Write Down Your Early Thoughts about the Material

Pianists do finger exercises before they play; baseball players take batting practice before a game. These activities help them limber up for the real thing. Similar exercises will help you prepare to write.

After a lecture or a discussion in a section, write down all the questions that come to your mind about what has been said. When you read, write down not only brief summaries of important information or vital thoughts in the text itself, but ask yourself questions. (I scribble copious notes and questions in the margins of all my own books. But NEVER, NEVER write in a library book!) I keep a separate notebook for every project I'm working on at a given time, using the blank books available now in most bookstores. You can carry a notebook in your book bag and jot down ideas. Ideas come to you in the strangest places, and if you make a habit of jotting them down when they hit, they will hit you more often. You can write on 3- by 5-inch cards, on yellow pads, or even on a computer. I find notebooks easier to carry around and easier to write in on the spur of the moment.

The main point is to jot down ideas about several possible topics unless some idea has already struck you with such force that you know you will write about it. Ask as many questions as you can when you survey your sources. Write these questions in your notebook. Set down your thoughts about the topic. As you go on in this random, almost playful writing, several things may happen.

You may become more aware of your own interests.

You may define and then refine your topic.

You may start assembling some evidence for your paper.

You may start shaping the argument that you will make in your paper.

It's usually good to start writing soon after you get an assignment. Don't make this preliminary writing a rough draft. Simply set down your thoughts, perhaps in disconnected paragraphs that allow you to work out some of your ideas. You may even write a series of sentences without trying to work them into paragraphs. You may just ramble about various aspects of your subject.

Inexperienced writers often assume that a writer does all the research first and then writes. The writing process falls then into neat blocks: One learns; one writes. On the contrary, most experienced writers find that no matter how much they know about a subject at the start, the act of writing itself stimulates them to ask new questions, to pursue new leads, and even to come to conclusions different from those they earlier assumed to be the fruits of their research. For the experienced writer, the writing proceeds in a process of leaping forward and then leaping back. Such a process may be diagramed like this:

I. Getting an idea

II. Preliminary investigation
   A. Writing some preliminary notes including thoughts and questions.

III. More investigation
   A. Writing more notes, perhaps a rough outline of the paper the writer intends to write. More questions.

IV. More investigation
   A. A first draft that reveals to the writer the shape of his or her thoughts, new questions to ask, gaps or fuzziness in what the writer knows.

V. More investigation
   A. A second draft that begins to look fairly complete, though it may even yet reveal some more questions.

VI. More investigation
   A. A final draft.

Different writers proceed in different ways. The process outlined here is typical, but it is not the only one. Now and then everyone can grasp a topic so thoroughly after one round of careful research and note taking that all that remains is to set the notes out on the table and write the paper. That is a relatively rare event.

To postpone writing until one has done all the possible research on the subject can be disastrous. Many historians have frustrated themselves and those who had great expectations of them by assuming that they had to read one more book or gather one more bit of information before they could start writing. That was the fate of Frederick Jackson Turner, who, after propounding his "frontier thesis" of American history, was expected to write important books on the subject. He signed several contracts with publishers without ever being able to produce the books. Historian Richard Hofstadter wrote the following sad words about Turner; they should be stamped on the skin of every historian tempted to put off writing.

He became haunted by the suspicion, so clear to his biographer, that he was temperamentally "incapable of the sustained effort necessary to complete a major scholarly volume." "I hate to write," he blurted out to a student in later years, "it is almost impossible for me to do so." But it was a self-description arrived at after long and hard experience. In 1901 when he was forty, Turner had signed contracts for nine books, not one of which was ever to be written and only a few of which were even attempted, and his life was punctuated by an endless correspondence with disappointed publishers. For an academic family, the Turners lived expensively and entertained generously, and the income from any of the textbooks he promised to write would have been welcome, but the carrot of income was no more effective than the stick of duty and ambition. Turner's teaching load at Wisconsin was for a time cut down, in the hope that it would clear the way for his productive powers, but what it produced was only a misunderstanding with university trustees. Turner's reluctance to address himself to substantive history was so overwhelming that A. B. Hart, a martinet of an editor who presided with ruthless energy over the authors of the American Nation series, extracted *Rise of the New West* out of him only by dint of an extraordinary series of nagging letters and bullying telegrams. Hart in the end counted this his supreme editorial achievement. "It ought to be carved on my tombstone that I was the only man in the world that secured what might be called an adequate volume from Turner," he wrote to Max Farrand; and Farrand, one of Turner's closest friends who watched his agonized efforts to produce his last unfinished volume in the splendid setting provided by the Huntington Library, sadly concluded that he would not have finished it had he lived forever.

Over the years Turner had built up a staggering variety of psychological and mechanical devices, familiar to all observers of academia, to stand between himself and the finished task. There was, for example, a kind of perfectionism, which sent him off looking for one more curious fact or decisive bit of evidence, and impelled the elaborate rewriting of drafts that had already been rewritten. There were the hopelessly optimistic plans for what he would do in the next two or twelve or eighteen months, whose inevitable nonfulfillment brought new lapses into paralyzing despair. There was an undisciplined curiosity, an insatiable, restless interest in *everything*, without a correspondingly lively determination to consummate anything; a flitting from one subject to another, a yielding to the momentary pleasures of research as a way of getting further from the discipline of writing. ("I have a lot of fun exploring, getting lost and getting back, and telling my companions about it," he said, but "telling" here did not mean writing.) There was overresearch and overpreparation with the consequent inability to sort out the important from the trivial—a small mountain of notes, for example, gathered for a trifling projected chldren's book of 25,000 words on George Rogers Clark. There were, for all the unwritten books, thirty-four large file drawers bulging with notes on every aspect of American history. There were elaborate maps, drawn to correlate certain forces at work in American politics. There were scrapbooks, and hours spent filling them in. . . . There were, of course, long letters of explanation to publishers, and other letters setting forth new plans for books. There was indeed an entire set of letters to Henry Holt and Company, examining various possible titles for the last unfinishable volume—letters that the exasperated publishers finally cut off by suggesting that the matter might well wait until the book itself became a reality.[1]

I have said in a previous chapter that most writers discover a remarkable stimulus to the mind in writing. Ideas begin to flow as the hand grips the pen or taps on the keyboard. It may have something to do with hand-brain coordination. Whatever it is, writers discover that their minds start acting so rapidly as they write that they can scarcely set down everything they think about a subject. You may think you do not have a lot to say about a subject. But as you start writing what you know and what you want to know, you may discover that you have more to say than you thought. That in turn will give you confidence to continue. All writers face these nagging questions: Do I really have anything to say? Is this hard work worth the effort? Will anyone ever be interested in this? By starting to put down your ideas early, you learn to answer these questions in the affirmative.

Here are some questions that someone wanting to write a paper on Woodrow Wilson might write after some preliminary reading and perhaps after hearing some lectures about Wilson in class:

What did people who knew Woodrow Wilson think of him?

Who supported him and who opposed him?

How did diplomats at the Paris Peace Conference in 1919 regard Wilson? What did they say about him in their memoirs?

---

[1]Richard Hofstadter, *The Progressive Historians,* New York, Knopf, 1968, pp. 115–117.

What were Wilson's relations with his Secretary of State, William Jennings Bryan?

What was Wilson's attitude toward blacks?

Who were the people closest to him?

Why did Wilson feel compelled to be the leader at the Peace Conference of 1919?

Why did people vote for him?

Where in the country did Wilson have his greatest support?

Where the least?

When did his popularity begin to wane?

When was his popularity at its height?

What was Wilson like in his own writing?

You can pursue your questions until you find one especially interesting to you. Your early questions will overlap. Don't worry about that. They make you think, and in time one will dominate your attention. You can then narrow your research to try to answer it. You cannot learn everything there is to know about Wilson in one term, and you certainly cannot write everything there is to write about Wilson in one paper. A series of good questions will eventually turn up one that will give you a direction for further inquiry.

II. LIMIT YOUR TOPIC

Our last paragraph brings us to an essential wisdom that every writer must learn. I have treated it extensively in the last chapter, but it needs to be repeated. In my experience the most common flaw in student papers about history is that the topics are so broad that the writers have no focus and cannot therefore develop an original idea. Keep these two points in mind:

1. Your topic must be defined narrowly enough to allow you to write an interesting, informative essay within the limits imposed by your assignment.

2. Your topic must be defined according to the sources available.

You cannot write an interesting and original paper entitled "Martin Luther" or "Abraham Lincoln" or "Woodrow Wilson" or "Susan B. Anthony." In 2000 or even 6000 words, you can only do a summary of the person's life—suitable, perhaps, for an encyclopedia article but not for a thoughtful essay that tries to make a special point. Pick a limited issue that you can study in depth and write about within the space you have available. People will believe you only if you give them some reason to believe you—some evidence. Compiling evidence takes time and careful development in the essay. By the time you have dealt with significant evidence, you will find yourself straining to keep within even a generous page limit.

Be sure you have access to sources for what you want to write. Students usually underestimate the sources available to them. A good prowl through your library as you are looking for a subject may reveal more than you dreamed was there. Reference librarians are my saints and heroes—professionals at finding things. Smart students and smart professors learn to talk to reference librarians about sources of information. Once when I was writing a carefully researched novel about going West in the year 1851, I asked a reference librarian at the University of Tennessee how someone might have amputated an injured arm on the Western plains at that time. She immediately led me to a little book called *Gunn's Domestic Medicine*, published in 1831. It provided complete and optimistic instructions. I had one of my characters follow those directions, and several doctors told me when the book was published how surprised they were that I knew so much about limbs and amputations. I gave the credit to the librarian.

Interlibrary loans can bring in books from all over the country, usually for a nominal fee and sometimes for nothing. Computer technology is growing exponentially even as I write, and materials available on CD-ROM are amazing in quantity and variety. Early in 1994 *The New York Times* reported that the CD-ROM revolution was just beginning; who can tell where it will be by the time this book is published! Reference librarians will know: Ask them.

Don't write a paper if you do not have access to the sources you need. If you try to write about the attitude of Woodrow Wilson toward black Americans, you will be hard-pressed to do so if you cannot study the huge Princeton edition of Wilson's works. If you want to write about the early development of printing, you will have a hard time if your library does not have some examples, at least on micro-film, of early printing. When you cannot find adequate sources, you cannot write an adequate paper. But your first step is to see what is there; then you can redefine your paper to fit the available sources.

III. DO RESEARCH

When you do research you do several steps:

You consult sources.

You formulate a thesis that helps you interpret those sources.

You weigh the sources to decide which are most important to your pur-pose. That is, you look at the sources critically to see what evidence they may contain for and against your thesis.

You organize the evidence to tell as accurately as possible the story you want to tell.

You put a design on the information so that it makes an essay.

You cite the sources to let readers know where you have gotten your in-formation.

Remember my earlier advice. Given the linear way in which I have described the steps in research, you may think that historians in-variably follow these steps neatly one after the other. Not so! In prac-tice things seldom run so smoothly. Historians may begin with one topic, discover another when they do research, and change their minds again at least in part when they start writing. As they write, they may go back and redefine their topic considerably, and as they redefine the topic they must do more research. Writing often reveals gaps in our knowledge that drive us back to do more research.

Start in the Reference Room

Start your research in the reference room of your library. A very good first step is to read several encyclopedia articles related to the subject you think might provide a good paper. Consult the most recent edition of several encyclopedias, though older editions may be enlighten-ing about scholarly opinions when they were published. If you look up the same subject in a multitude of different reference works, many essential facts about your topic will be stamped in your memory. If in an American history course you decide that you might like to do a pa-per on President Woodrow Wilson, read five or six encyclopedia arti-cles about him. Read some from old editions of encyclopedias pub-lished during his life and others from more recent editions published after his death. You will then have different perspectives on his career as well as background knowledge of many events in his life.

Your reference room will have the standard general encyclope-dias—the multivolume sets such as *Britannica, Americana,* and *Collier's,* and the single-volume encyclopedias such as *The New Columbia Encyclopedia* and the *Random House Encyclopedia.* Look also into the reference works that may be specifically addressed to your field of inquiry. You may choose a topic related to religion. *The New Catholic Encyclopedia* in fifteen volumes provides a treasury of modern scholarship on religious figures and religious movements of all sorts. (*The Catholic Encyclopedia,* which *The New Catholic Encyclopedia* replaced, will probably be in the stacks of your library; it is still extremely useful, though written in a less sprightly manner than the newer version.) *The New Standard Jewish Encyclopedia* pro-vides a similar source for the history of the Jewish people and Judaism. It is enlightening to read the articles on, say, Martin Luther, in these works. All these articles will have brief bibliographies at the end listing some of the standard works where you can find more in-formation on the subject.

The International Encyclopedia of the Social Sciences in nineteen volumes provides much information on issues interesting to histori-ans. *The Social Science Encyclopedia,* published in one thick volume in 1985 and edited by Adam Kuper and Jessical Kuper, is a mine of recent scholarship on social studies. *The Funk and Wagnalls Standard Dictionary of Folklore, Mythology and Legend* in two volumes will give you information about beliefs prevalent in many societies. *The Encyclopedia of World Art* in fifteen volumes is filled with informa-tion about artists, particular works of art, museums, patrons, and the subjects of art. *The New Grove Dictionary of Music* in twenty vol-umes does much the same thing with music, so that if you want to know something about how Luther figured in art you can look him up in one, and in music, the other.

Many reference books are designed especially for historians. The American Historical Association's *Guide to Historical Literature*, last published in 1961, is out of date now, but it gives a good account of works in history published before that date. The multivolume *Cambridge Ancient History, The Cambridge Mediaeval History*, and *The New Cambridge Modern History* are filled with authoritative articles, sometimes written without much verve but still worthwhile. *The Harvard Guide to American History* in two volumes is useful. The *Dictionary of National Biography* is indispensable for any work on British history. *The Dictionary of American Biography* is much inferior, but one can find there interesting information about important Americans who may be subjects of historical research. Many librarians have old nineteenth-century biographical encyclopedias, and these are not to be scorned. Many people well known in their time who have dropped into oblivion since will be found there.

Don't hesitate to use current works in foreign languages in your reference room. Even if you do not read the language, you may discover illustrations or other useful materials. If you have had a year or two of study in the language, you may discover that you can read the materials far better than you suspected. That discovery may draw you into further use of it—an advantage to the student of history, where knowledge of foreign languages is essential to advanced work in nearly all the historical fields.

Bibliographies

Always compile a bibliography while you are doing research. Start early, and you will save yourself much grief. You can jot down titles in a notebook or on 3- by 5-inch cards. If you begin in the reference room of your library, note the full bibliographic references both to the articles you read and to the recommendations for further reading in the bibliographies appended to those articles. Look up your subject and related subjects in the card catalog of your library. Your library probably now has a computerized catalog for looking up the titles and authors of books as well as subjects and key words of titles. Consult books and articles that include bibliographies and notes. In all the places where other scholars have done research on your subject or on subjects related to yours, you will find titles. Be sure you study the journals in the field you write about. Now let's consider these steps one at a time.

Primary Sources: Editions of Complete and Selected Works

Be on the lookout for editions of the written works of the various people who may enter your paper. Using texts written by those you write about gives your own work authority. When you use any edition of collected or selected works, check the dates of publication. Sometimes several different editions have been published of the same works; usually, but not always, the best editions are the latest. These editions may be of different sorts. The most valuable are editions of the complete works, in which every surviving text is collected and indexed, sometimes with other materials.

The most valuable source for a paper on Woodrow Wilson would be the great Princeton edition of his complete papers edited by Arthur Link and others. Use the indexes in such editions. For example, if you become interested in Wilson's attitudes toward black Americans, look in the index to see both where blacks are mentioned in general and what particular black leaders are mentioned. (In the Princeton edition of Wilson's works, entries for black Americans are found under the heading "Negroes.") The papers of presidential confidants and government servants are often published. The papers of Edward Mandell House, long a confidant of President Wilson, have been published. Political papers of many sorts in various foreign countries may be published, and you should examine the card catalog in your library to see if any of these editions are available to you. David Lloyd George, Prime Minister of Great Britain at the end of World War I, published a large autobiography in which he spoke frequently—and critically—of Wilson. If you write about the attitude toward Wilson of various heads of state with whom he worked, consult Lloyd George's work. As your knowledge of people around Wilson enlarges, you can consult the library or bibliographies in encyclopedia articles about these people to see what books they wrote. Complete editions of the works of writers and historical figures are also widely available. The works of Benjamin Franklin, James Boswell, and Thomas More have been rolling off the presses of Yale University for several decades now. Almost every large university press is involved in publishing somebody's complete works. Often these editions come with long and informative introductory essays and extended commentaries. In *The Yale Edition of the Complete Works of St. Thomas More,* every quotation More gives from the works of another writer, ancient or otherwise, has been either located or else noted as being unfound. Nearly all of them have been found. Indexes to each volume make finding various topics and names easy, although indexes vary in usefulness. The Toronto edition of the works of Erasmus in English translation offers a similar wealth of information in its notes, as does the Latin edition of Erasmus's works (he wrote only in Latin) that is a joint Dutch-English publishing venture. An excellent way of writing a paper for almost any course is to find an edition of the works of someone studied in the course, to read in that edition for a time, and to discover some subject that makes you curious. Sometimes editions of selected works are available. The danger of selected works is obvious; the selection depends on the judgments of editors working in a certain time and a certain place, and what is important to them may be less important to later generations.

Editions of correspondence are common. Most of us love to read letters because, like photographs, they give us a sense of intimacy with bygone times and people we have not known. Like photographs, letters are quickly datable. One quickly sees that they belong to a certain time and a certain place, and so in the eternal flux of things, they seem to make time stand still for a moment. Collections of correspondence give us figures in relatively unguarded prose, commenting on daily life often without the caution that marks more public utterances. The private persona or personality of the letter writer may be different from the public image displayed in speeches or writings intended for a large audience. Cicero's writings on various subjects such as old age reveal an attractive man, removed from self-seeking and pettiness. His letters often give an opposite view. Letters may also provide factual information unavailable elsewhere. Published diaries are often available, and unpublished diaries—usually in the original form in which they were written—abound in many library collections. If your library has a manuscript collection, you may find unpublished manuscript diaries there.

Many people write autobiographies—the most untrustworthy of historical sources because of the natural desire of the writers to put themselves in the best possible light for posterity. Still autobiographies are there, and all of them contain some truth—though some are more truthful than others.

Often editions of various sources relating to a general topic are also collected and published. One of the most monumental of these collections is *The War of the Rebellion; A Compilation of the Official*

Records of the Union and Confederate Armies, published in seventy volumes and containing, it seems, a record of almost every scrap of paper exchanged within the armies of both sides in the Civil War. (The noise of battle during the Civil War was so tremendous that people could not hear each other speak; therefore written orders carried from place to place on the battlefield were much more common than in earlier wars, and thousands of these were collected by the editors of *The War of the Rebellion. The Calendar of State Papers, Spanish* includes English translations of all the letters exchanged between the Spanish ambassadors in London and their sovereigns at home during much of the sixteenth century, and so constitutes an edition of documents, not all by the same author. Generations of historians have used *Documents Illustrative of English Church History,* edited by Henry Gee and William John Hardy in one large volume and published in 1921. These and many others that could be listed are examples of collections that may help you in your research.

Whatever your topic, check to see if there might be a collection of published documents related to your paper. More recent editions are usually better than the older ones. The discipline of scholarly editing is difficult, its techiques demanding, and its technology constantly changing and improving.

Secondary Sources

The bibliographies in the articles you read in reference works will give you a start toward both the primary sources for your study and the secondary sources. The secondary sources will broaden your understanding and help you see the problems and opportunities in the sources as other writers have seen them.

Books

Secondary sources will be of two general sorts—books and articles. A few bibliographies are annotated; that is, the compiler offers a brief comment on the books and articles he or she has noted:

> Contamine, Philippe, *War in the Middle Ages,* trans. Michael Jones, New York, Basil Blackwell, 1986. A lively account of how wars were fought from the barbarian age to the Renaissance. Not only in-

cludes an analysis of tactics and strategy but also discusses various theological and ethical attitudes toward war. Illustrated with both photographs and diagrams.

An annotated bibliography may be unreliable; the writer may judge some books too harshly, some too generously. But such a bibliography will usually provide worthwhile information about the contents of books and articles.

You can often locate books about your subject more quickly than you can find articles. The reason is simple; the titles of books show up in the catalog of your library and articles do not. (Thanks to computer indexing, articles are much easier to locate than they once were; in the next section, I'll tell you how to find them.)

The card catalog in your library will list books under subject headings and by author. Under "Wilson, Woodrow," you will find biographies of Wilson and other books that have Wilson as a major subject, as well as books Wilson wrote himself. The alphabetical listing of books by their authors may list several titles by the same scholar. Because historians tend to specialize, several books by one author may be related to your inquiry. Another excellent way of locating books is to go into the stacks of your library and look at the volumes classified in one section. Many different books about Woodrow Wilson will be on the same shelf.

The footnotes or endnotes of books and articles can serve as references to other scholarly works about your subject. Don't limit yourself to books about Woodrow Wilson; look for books that deal with his times. You may consult books about World War I, about the progressive era that he represented, about people close to Wilson, and about various issues in which he was involved. In such works you would look up the name "Wilson, Woodrow" in the index and turn to those pages to see how Wilson is mentioned. You might discover yourself on the trail of a valuable insight.

Articles

Hundreds of periodicals deal with history. Some publish articles on particular facets of history—the Middle Ages, military history, history of science, art history, and so on. Some have a scope as wide as the discipline of history itself. An afternoon spent consulting the annual indexes of bound periodicals can open your eyes to many issues that touch on your subject. New interpretations and information about any discipline usually get into print first in articles. To stay on top of a field, you must consult the periodical literature.

Academic titles usually are fairly straightforward—often a catchy phrase followed by a colon and an explanatory subtitle. When you consult an index, you can quickly find articles of interest. Your library will have an index for all the periodicals it takes. You will usually find it in the periodical room. Here are a few historical journals you might wish to consult. The list is by no means complete; I include it only to provide a start in your own efforts. Looking at these journals will help you see how vast periodical literature can be. Since the essays you write in a history course are more like journal articles than books, the journals will provide models of writing and thinking that you can imitate.

Your reference room will almost certainly have *The American Historical Review,* the journal published by the American Historical Association, to which most professors of history belong. Don't be misled by the title of the periodical; it is not limited to topics about American history. The *AHR,* as the title is usually abbreviated, carries articles about all aspects of history in all the regions of the world. The journal *Past and Present* carries many diverse articles about history. *The English Historical Review* includes articles from the entire range of history, and one is likely to see an essay on early modern China just before another on nineteenth-century America. *The Historical Journal,* also published in England, strives for a similar breadth. The *The Journal of Modern History* does not carry articles about the period before 1500, and most of its authors consider topics from the eighteenth century to the recent past.

Regional journals abound. *The Journal of the West* is specialized, carrying articles dealing with the history of that part of the United States that lies west of the Mississippi River. Another regional periodical is *The Journal of Southern History,* which treats the southeastern United States, the region of the old Confederacy. *The Tennessee Historical Quarterly* will narrow the field even further, treating topics dealing with the state of Tennessee. Every state in the United States has at least one journal devoted to its own history, and many large cities have historical societies that publish a regular journal or occasional monographs.

The Journal of American Culture is specialized in a different way; there you are likely to read about popular culture, and you may see articles on television commercials and on the history of comic books. *Church History* is specialized in still another way, featuring scholarly articles about the history of Christianity around the world. *The Catholic Historical Review* includes articles about the same field, and despite its title, often carries essays about Protestants and Protestant theology.

How to Find Relevant Articles

These titles represent only a tiny percentage of journals published in history. In this mass of publication, how do you find the articles that may pertain to your subject? I have counseled looking for sources in the notes and bibliographies of books that have been written about your topic. Outstanding articles get read and quoted and often appraised by other scholars. Pay attention to those footnotes or endnotes where a writer mentions the literature related to the subject. I mentioned earlier that searching the annual indexes of historical periodicals is an excellent way to find articles on your topic. While searching for articles on Luther's ideas about justification by faith in the indexes of *The Journal of Modern History*, you may run across Jean Wirth's review article of 1985 in which he surveys the major works on Luther published to commemorate the 500th anniversary of the birth of the German reformer in 1483. Wirth's wisdom, wit, and comprehensiveness will give you an insight into modern Luther scholarship that you might not have seen otherwise.

Book reviews in historical journals provide another valuable source of bibliographic information. Most journals publish reviews, usually in the back of the issue. These are written by specialists in the various fields. Journals may classify the books reviewed by historical period or by subject. You can easily locate the books published about the time period that interests you most.

Reviews vary widely in their value; some are impressionistic, some bad-tempered and malicious, some far too gentle or laudatory, and some cursory summaries. But a review by a widely published expert in the field may provide a good appraisal of the strengths and weaknesses of the book—although sometimes experts have a tin ear to radically new and important developments in their fields. Very often a good reviewer will mention another book or article relating to the theme of the book immediately under review. By reading reviews you can pick up information about the field itself that you might otherwise miss, and you can find bibliographic references that will help you find books and articles relevant to your topic. If you read seven or eight reviews of the same book, you will get a pretty good idea of how specialists in the field regard it.

Of great value are the indexes to periodical literature to be found in all good libraries. The most common of these and the best known is *The Reader's Guide to Periodical Literature,* which has been regularly published since 1900. Updates appear throughout the year, and at the end of each year a large, comprehensive edition is published. *The Reader's Guide* surveys only magazines intended for a general audience. Don't scorn this purpose, for you may find interesting, well-written articles by important specialists by consulting *The Reader's Guide.* You will not find articles published in the specialized journals and intended for professional historians, articles most likely to provide the information and the interpretations you need in a paper intended for a history class.

Fortunately the computer has come to the rescue. *The Permuterm Subject Index* and *Citation Index* for the arts and humanities and for the social sciences are now essential tools for every working historian. The indexes are issued annually and updated halfway through each year. Here one may find the name of every author who has published an article in many specialized journals surveyed by the editors. One may find a listing of every significant word that has appeared in every title of the articles surveyed, these words arranged so that one may rapidly locate articles related to one's field of inquiry. If you were looking up material on Woodrow Wilson, you would find in these indexes the title of every article that included the words *Woodrow Wilson.* If you were looking up material on the Great Depression of the 1930s, these indexes would include every title that included the word *Depression.* Full bibliographic information is given for each article, and every source mentioned in the footnotes or endnotes of the article is also listed. The result is a splendidly usable guide that will allow you to find quickly and easily the latest scholarly articles on the subject you are pursuing. Complete, clear instructions for the use of the Permuterm indexes are in the front of each volume. If you have trouble getting the hang of it, your reference librarian can help you. Permuterm has just gone on CD-ROM disks.

Almost as spectacular is the computer index called *America History and Life,* published annually in three volumes, one being article abstracts and citations, one an index to book reviews in American history, and the third an American history bibliography. Abstracts are valuable wherever you find them; they summarize the argument of an article, leaving you the option to seek the article out and read it for yourself. These computer index publications do not yet include articles published before computer indexing began in the early 1980s. But compilation of computer indexed bibliographies in various fields has become an academic industry, changing and growing constantly. Various firms are putting older material on computer software, especially CD-ROM, with as much zeal as publishing businesses in the 1950s and 1960s put old books and newspapers on microfilm. Your reference librarian can help you locate firms that will provide a computer-generated bibliography for almost any subject. Prices and quality vary, but the technology is improving all the time, and this sort of bibliographic aid will soon become a common and indispensable tool for historical researchers.

Unpublished Materials

Most history papers are written from printed sources. But do not dismiss the possibility of using other kinds of information. Many libraries include archives that house collections of unpublished papers of immense richness and variety. Why was a certain building constructed on your campus? Why was your college founded? Why did the founders locate it where they did? How did a nineteenth-century college president at your institution construe the job? Answers to these and other questions may be found in letters, journals, memos, and other materials available to you if you take the trouble to find them in the archives. Ask your librarian if your school archives are open to students.

Many libraries now include oral history collections, tapes and records of people well known and obscure discussing the past and their participation in events then. You can learn something by the tone of voice people use to describe past events. A comparison between someone's oral recollections of an event and written accounts can make an interesting topic for a paper.

Interviews are valuable for studies of recent or fairly recent history. If you are writing about some aspect of World War II, you can find many veterans to tell you of their experiences, giving you a first-hand view of history. The same is true of the civil rights movement, the Vietnam War, the Great Depression, and other events of the past fifty or so years. The definition of your topic will help you decide whether such interviews are helpful. People who participated in great events are often eager to talk about them. Don't be afraid to call people up to ask for an interview.

Be sure to prepare for the interview by learning all you can about the person and by writing out questions beforehand, but don't be mechanically bound to your list once the interview begins. Explore each question thoroughly. Listen to what your source says and be prepared to ask for clarification or for details.

The pleasures of all these methods of inquiry are immense. Historians who have worked in the archives or who have heard the actual voices of witnesses to history in the making experience a pleasure that can hardly be described. Reading one of Henry David Thoreau's essays in manuscript, looking at his handwriting, and holding the paper that he held when he wrote, are all special delights to the person writing about Thoreau.

To some it is even more moving to hold the letters or other papers written by people much more obscure, people forgotten except for some striking personal imprint of themselves left in writing. Both Yale University and the Huntington Library in California have large collections of diaries kept by people who went across the western plains in covered wagons or on foot in the mid-nineteenth century. Sometimes a reader can see the stains left by a rain that fell over a century ago, and one can often tell something about the difficulty of the journey by noticing the changes in the handwriting. At some point every student of history, whether the amateur or the professional, should have the pleasure of looking at such a source.

Taking Notes

Both the gathering of titles and your later reading of these books and articles will require you to take notes. Take scratch notes as you do your preliminary reading. Ask yourself questions, jot down significant phrases, and perhaps note the places where historians disagree on the subject you are pursuing. Note what concerns one historian and does not concern another. One writer may write much about Luther's hatred of the Jews; one may write little or nothing on that subject. Jot these different opinions down. Jot down your own opinions, too. Even in the early stages of your research, important ideas may pop into your head. Write them down. Test them with further study. You will often discover that further research will prove that some of your first impressions are gems.

Computers add facility to note taking. If you copy your notes into a computer file, you can locate key words by using the search function on your word processing program. Most programs will allow you to shift your notes to the file holding your essay when you start your writing. For larger projects, data base programs allow even more variety in the way you preserve and retrieve your notes.

Review your notes at the end of each day. Many students take notes and then do not go back over them later on. Our short-term memory is flighty. You can read something, be intensely engaged in it, and take notes about it—but then forget it quickly if you do not do something to renew the experience. Reviewing notes fixes them in your mind and makes you remember them better so that you find them easily among your thoughts when you start to write. Reviewing your scratch notes will help you hold onto ideas that will then be nurtured by your subconscious powers of incubation, the almost miraculous ability of the mind to work while thinking of other things or even sleeping. Reading the notes over again will stir up thoughts that will contribute much to the final conception of your paper, and such reading will clarify the method you use to approach that goal.

The Forms of Notes

Always include bibliographical references in your notes. For books, write down the name of the author, the title of the book, the place of publication, usually the publisher, and the date of publication. For articles, include the name of the author, the title of the article, the title of the journal, its volume number (if any), the date (if any), and the year in which the article appears together with the page numbers of the article.

Hyatt, Irwin T., <u>Our Ordered Lives Confess,</u> Cambridge, Mass. and London, England, Harvard University
Press, 1976.

Later on, you can refer in your notes simply to "Hyatt, p. 27" to
locate your source of information. If you cite several books or articles
by the same author, give the author and an abbreviated form of the title for your notes. Instead of giving the full bibliographic information
for Woodrow Wilson's *History of the American People,* you can say,
"Wilson, *History,* 4 (to indicate the fourth volume in the set), p. 160."
You can, of course, use other systems. The main principle is this: Be
sure you know where you got your information. You must be able to
refer accurately to your sources when you write your paper. You will
save yourself much grief if you keep track of them carefully while you
do your research.

In addition to your bibliographic notes, you will take three kinds
of notes as you read. The first is direct quotation. Always place direct
quotations within quotation marks in your notes, and copy the quotations accurately. Make an accurate reference to the page number or
numbers of the book where the quotation is found. You may want to
put a heading on the note to help you remember why you set it down,
and, if you use a computer, to help you find the note by means of the
search function on your word processing program. Here is an example:

Civil War Nursing role of women; Kate Cumming:
"Nothing that I had ever heard of or read had given me
the faintest idea of the horrors witnessed here[;]. . . I
sat up all night, bathing the men's wounds, and giving
them water. . . . The men are lying all over the house,
on their blankets, just as they were brought in from
the battlefield. . . . The foul air from this mass of human beings at first made me giddy and sick, but I soon
got over it. We have to walk, and when we give the men
anything kneel, in blood and water, but we think nothing of it." Selections from Kate Cumming's diary,
telling of her work with wounded Confederate soldiers.
Quoted from James M. McPherson, <u>Battle Cry of Freedom:</u>

The Civil War Era, New York, Oxford University Press,
1988, p. 479.

A search through your computer file of notes would pick up "Civil
War Nursing," "women," "Kate Cumming," and of course any of the
words in the quoted section. Always review the quotation for accuracy
once you have written it down to see that you have it correct. The eye
and the hand can slip while you are looking first at your source and
then at your notebook or card. When you type, fingers can go astray,
typing one word when you meant another. It may help to put a little
check mark by the quotation to tell yourself that you have reviewed
the quotation for accuracy once you have written it down.

Here is another sample note showing direct quotation:

Wilson mocks blacks' fear of the Klan/KKK
"It threw the negroes into a very ecstasy of panic
to see these sheeted 'ku klux' move near them in the
shrouded night; and their comic fear stimulated the
lads who excited it to many an extravagant prank and
mummery. No one knew or could discover who the masked
players were; no one could say whether they meant serious or only innocent mischief; and the zest of the
business lay in keeping the secret close." Wilson, History, 5, pp. 59-60.

If this note were on your computer and you wished to retrieve it
as an example of Wilson's attitude toward the Ku Klux Klan, you could
search it on the computer by using "Klan" or "KKK" in your heading.
The note would also be easy to retrieve if you wrote it in a notebook.

Avoid copying too much as direct quotation. Writing down the
quotation takes time, and you can easily make errors in transcribing
the quotation from source to note. You can save time and help your
own mental processes if you summarize or paraphrase material rather
than quoting it directly. Paraphrasing is especially valuable if your
source is in a foreign language or in a language with a difficult syntax
such as early modern English.

As you write, you will probably have Wilson's volumes at hand
that you have checked out of the library. When looking at your note,
you may decide to return to the original source and quote it *verbatim,*

that is, word for word. Or, to save space, you may say something like
this: "Wilson mocked the fear blacks had of the Klan," and you would
put in a note of the place where the mockery might be found. Here is
an example of a summary note:

Wilson mocks black fears of Klan/KKK. Wilson seems
to enjoy the fear of blacks before the Ku Klux Klan and
seemed to regard the early Klansmen as mere pranksters.
Wilson, History, 5, pp. 59-60.

The third kind of note is your own comment as you read. Try to
comment often as you take notes. As you write such comments, you
force your mind to reflect on what you read. Commenting on your
reading makes you an active rather than a passive reader. *Be sure to
distinguish between the notes that are your own thoughts and notes
that are direct quotations or summaries of your sources.* I usually put
an arrow before one of my thoughts in my notebook or when I am
taking notes on a computer. The arrow lets me know that these are
my thoughts, and that I am not taking them down from someone else.
Many notebook keepers write direct quotations on the right-hand
page and keep their own comments on the left-hand page.

Here is an example of how you would enter a note on a card
about your own thoughts. You would enter the note in a computer
without this indentation.

Wilson's view of the Klan goes hand in hand with his
general view that blacks have no right to be free of
fear or to take part as citizens in the United States.
His mention of the "comic" fear of blacks suggests an
unconscious appropriation of the common stereotypes,
that blacks were either funny or dangerous. He barely
suggests in the History that blacks are mistreated by
Southerners—including the Klansmen. They are always
mistreated by Northerners. Northerners always mistreat
them by asking them to assert themselves. Wilson sees
blacks as being most happy when they are submissive. He
seemed to have no sense of dignity that blacks might
lose by being so regarded. History, 5, pp. 59-60.

If you keep your mind active during your reading and make notes like this, you may find that you have a design for your paper in your hand before you sit down to write.

IV. BRAINSTORM AND MAKE AN OUTLINE

"Brainstorming" is the term we use for making the mind work at a task through a playful, intense forcing out of our thoughts. We may jot down ideas one after another as fast as we can think of them, knowing that we may reject most of them. We may brainstorm in groups by talking hard at each other, trying out ideas, tossing them out to the group to see how they fare in open discussion. Brainstorming is an excellent way of arriving at a topic for a history paper.

By the time you have spent two or three afternoons refining your subject, gathering bibliography, and doing some spot reading, you will begin to feel more confident about your knowledge. You will have left the somewhat flat and limited accounts of the encyclopedias and other reference books, and you will have started looking at primary sources and specialized books and articles. Your reading should have suggested several interesting topics. You should have asked questions along the way, writing those questions down in your notebook. You will have noticed some patterns or repeated ideas in the work of someone you are studying.

Sometimes a pattern occurs in a consistent response to certain subjects. Woodrow Wilson defended the South in writing and in speeches. Why did he do that, and what effect did this attitude have on American history? You may have started with the resolve to write a paper about Woodrow Wilson. If you were lucky, you thought of a limited topic right away, one you might do in ten or fifteen pages. Perhaps, however, you have not been able to limit your topic enough even now. Make a list of interesting topics or problems relating to Woodrow Wilson. Keep working at it until you arrive at something you can manage. The following notes illustrate this working to produce something both interesting and feasible.

"The Civil War in Woodrow Wilson's <u>History of the American People</u>" Too vague. Too many topics possible here.

"Wilson's Defense of the Ku Klux Klan" in his <u>History of the American People</u>." Not bad. Wilson's defense of the Klan is surprising, given the popular conception that Wilson was liberal for his time. But here the topic seems almost too narrow. Wilson defends the Klan over several pages in his book. He makes some vague comments that indicate disapproval of violence by the Klan. None of Wilson's <u>History</u> is very detailed. He makes general statements throughout, and the book serves much more to show what he felt and believed about the facts rather than what the facts were or might have been.

The temptation might be to go from Wilson to some general background information about the Klan itself. Then you have to ask questions like these: "Do I have primary sources to study the Klan? Is that topic far too big for a paper in my course?" Wilson's sympathetic words for the Klan provoke other ideas. What was Wilson's attitude toward blacks in the South and in society at large? Consult the index in several volumes of the Wilson papers. Slowly read Wilson's comments about blacks in various contexts. Here is much information, and you begin to see consistent patterns. Wilson has no sympathy for the efforts of blacks to vote after the Civil War. He never writes as if blacks might someday share white society as equals. He favors segregation in the federal civil service, especially the Post Office. He insults black leaders who come to visit him at the White House. The major pattern seems clear: Wherever Wilson speaks of race, he assumes the inferiority of blacks and aims at segregation.

Slowly a paper emerges. You adopt a provisional title: "Woodrow Wilson's Attitudes toward Black Americans." You can change a provisional title later. You can change anything in a paper, and your changes may be sweeping. While you use it, the provisional title gives direction to your work. That sense of direction will help you work faster and more efficiently because it helps organize your thoughts, making you evaluate the information you have collected so you can make proper use of it.

If you have done your research well, you cannot use all the information you have collected in your notes. Good writing is done out of an abundance of knowledge. The provisional title will act as a filter in your mind, holding and organizing things you should keep for your essay and letting go information that will not contribute to your argument.

The Outline

Once you arrive at a topic, focus your reading. If you plan to write about Woodrow Wilson's relation to blacks in America, limit yourself to reading only the parts of the Wilson papers and of books about Wilson relating to that subject. You may become so interested in Wilson that you continue to seek other information about him later on. Good! But while you write a paper, limit your reading to texts that help you to your goal.

You may write an outline to help organize your ideas and your evidence. Some writers sit down and start hammering on the keyboard without any clear idea where they are going. But it is usually more efficient to shape your ideas before you begin to write a draft. You can at least jot down a list of points you want to cover—a list that can be much more flexible than a detailed outline. You can rearrange items on your list as your intuitions suggest better forms of organization. Never be afraid to change a list or outline once you have begun. No matter how clearly you think you see your project in outline before you write a draft, writing may change your ideas. Be ready to follow your mind in its adventures with the evidence. Here is an example of an outline for a paper on Woodrow Wilson's attitudes toward black Americans:

The argument: Woodrow Wilson's attitudes towards blacks, a mixture of paternalism and fear, contributed to racial segregation introduced in the federal civil service early in his presidential administration.

1. William Monroe Trotter's interview with Wilson in November 1914 on the subject of segregation.
2. The larger meaning of the interview.
3. Wilson's reasons given to Trotter for accepting racial segregation.
4. The deeper explanation—Wilson's lifelong attitudes towards black Americans, attitudes ex-

pressed in things he said and wrote long before
he became President of the United States.

5. Origins: Wilson's romantic view of the South and
   his admiration for the old Confederacy.

6. The attitudes expressed in his History of the
   American People.

7. The hostility to blacks by white Southerners
   Wilson appointed to his cabinet.

8. Acceptance of racial segregation by the American
   people.

9. Wilson's segregationist policies and their disastrous effect on race relations in America.

A list outline such as this one avoids a proliferation of Roman numerals and subheadings. You may add subheadings if you want. Having made a list outline, you can write a first draft. You have decided, for example, to shape an analytical narrative. That is, you will tell a story and explain its significance for American history. You will tell what happened, who is responsible, and why the story is important. Along the way you will tell when and where these happenings took place. And so you can begin.

V. WRITE SEVERAL DRAFTS

Leave yourself time enough to do several drafts of your paper. If you don't start writing your paper until the day before it is due, stay up all night to do that first draft, and hand it in without having time to revise it, you rob yourself of the chance to do well. You may get by, but you may not be proud of your work. Note that I am not saying you should not stay up all night long working on your paper before you hand it in. Many writers discover that they get an adrenaline flow from working steadily at a final draft for hours and hours before they give it up, and they may stay up all night because they are excited about their work and cannot leave it. But no writer can produce consistently good work by waiting until the last minute to begin. Discipline yourself. When you start writing, stick to it for at least a couple of hours. You may not go very fast. You may consult your notes continually. You may become discouraged. But stay seated, and keep going. The most important task for you in writing your first draft is to get it into being. Get a beginning, a middle, and an end down on paper or on your computer. Write more than you need to write at first. If your assignment is to write a fifteen-page paper, make your first draft twenty pages. Pack in information. Use quotations. Ruminate about what you are describing. Ask yourself the journalistic questions, and try to answer them about your paper.

When you get your first draft into being, several things happen. You feel an immense relief. An unwritten assignment is more formidable than one you have written—even in a rough draft. You have some idea now what you can say in the space you have available. You have some idea of the major questions you want to address. You know some areas of weakness where you have to do further research. You can see which of your conclusions seem fairly certain and which seem shaky. You can see if you have an idea that binds all your data together into a thesis, a controlling motive that resolves or defines some puzzle that you find in your sources. You can now revise.

Revision proceeds in various ways. If you write with a computer and a word processing program, you can bring your paper up on the screen and start working back though it, inserting, deleting, and changing around the order of the paper. (It's a good idea to make a backup copy of that first draft so that if you cut something you decide you want to restore later on, you can do so without pain.) Many writers like to print out a draft and go over it with a pen or pencil, making changes that they then type into the draft on the computer. Some research has shown that the longer people work with computers, the more they tend to do their revising directly from the screen without printing out. I have written with computers now for thirteen years; I revise less and less from "hard copy," the printed page. I am revising this book by running it through my screen again and again, trying to make it shorter, more economical, more usable. The main task is to read your work over many times.

As you read, ask yourself questions. Here is my own list; you may add some of your own.

1. What is my major motive for writing this essay? What do I want to prove?

2. What would draw a modern reader to this essay? What audience do I want?

3. Do I quote, summarize, and paraphrase sources that support my point of view? Do I have evidence for my argument?

4. Do I provide enough context to allow readers less informed than I am to follow my essay easily? Can the essay stand alone for the generally educated reader?

5. Have I classified my evidence? That is, have I placed similar kinds of evidence in the same section of my paper so that readers will not have the feeling of being jerked randomly from one subject to another?

6. Where do I infer conclusions from the evidence? That is, where do I interpret the evidence instead of being content merely to report it?

7. Do I take contrary evidence into account? Have I been fair in my presentation of the evidence? Have I written in such a way that someone who knows the evidence as well as I do can compliment me for having done a careful job of putting everything together?

8. Are my transitions effective? Are the sections of my paper fitted together clearly enough to allow readers to move easily from one to the next without losing track of my argument? Or is there a digression, a jump from one idea to another without adequate preparation?

9. Is my opening interesting enough to draw readers even if they are not specialists in the subject?

10. Does my conclusion mirror my opening in some way? (A good essay comes back to the beginning when it concludes. Some words or ideas that drew attention in the first paragraph are repeated in the last. The beginning points toward the end, and by repeating some of the ideas in the beginning, the writer announces the conclusion. Usually one can read the first and last paragraphs of an essay and have a fairly good idea of what the essay is about and the point of view of the writer.)

11. What is my tone in this paper? Do I sound emotional or preachy? Do I sound belligerent? Do I sound apologetic? Do I sound immature?

12. Are there muddled sentences in this draft? Are my sentences clear enough to be understood at first reading? Can I make some of them more simple by eliminating cumbersome phrases or clauses?

13. Can I eliminate words, phrases, sentences, or whole paragraphs? Must every word I have used be there if I am to express the meaning I want? Can I cut out unnecessary information?

14. Can I make some sentences more vivid by using the active rather than the passive voice?

15. Do I repeat some words or phrases too often? Can I find other words and phrases to give variety to my prose? Are there echoes in my prose that I can change? That is, do I say things like, "The defendant defended himself," or "The writer wrote," or "Her description described," or "They considered all the considerations in the statement"?

16. Have I used clichés, those tired expressions used so often that they have lost all power to be vivid? Have I talked about "the cold, hard facts," a "bolt from the blue," someone "dead as a doornail," the "bottom line," or the "stark reality"?

As I have already said, you can cultivate a good sense of revision by reading your own work again and again. Reading aloud helps. You can sometimes pick out rough places in your prose because they make you stumble in the reading. Reading aloud with a certain amount of inflection and expression will help you catch places where you may be misleading or confusing.

Professional writers often have others read their work and make suggestions about it. Get help from friends. Don't ask them, "What do you think of my paper?" They will tell you it's good. Ask them instead, "What do you think I am saying in this paper?" You will sometimes be surprised by what comes out—and you will have some ideas for revision.

For most of us, the drafting process goes on until the last minute. Drafting helps us see all parts of our work more clearly. It helps us see our thinking, our research, our factual knowledge, our expression, and the shape of our ideas. Very often as we write drafts we realize that our thought is flabby or we suddenly discover contrary arguments. We revise to take these contrary arguments into account. Reading our work over and over again teaches us to track our own ideas so that we make them flow from one to another without leaving gaps that may hinder readers from making the connections we want them to make.

5

A Sample Research Paper in History

Here is a sample history paper written for a course in American history using the process outlined in Chapter 4. Study the paper. Then study the questions about the paper at the end. You may use these questions for any article you read about history or for any paper you write.

    Pay close attention to the format of the paper. Note the title page, the footnotes, and the bibliography. The title page includes the title of the paper, the name of the author, the date the paper is turned in, the name of the course, the time of the class, and the name of the professor. The margins should be set at 1 inch on all four sides of the page. ALWAYS number pages.

Woodrow Wilson's Attitudes Toward Black Americans

By Dick Curry

November 14, 1994
American History 221
Professor Archibald Rutledge
MWF 10:00-11:00

1

On November 12, 1914, William Monroe Trotter and
President Woodrow Wilson confronted each other in the
White House. Trotter was a leader in the struggle of
black Americans to end racial discrimination in the
United States. He read the president an "Address" vigorously protesting the policy of racial segregation recently introduced into the federal civil service, especially the United States Post Office. At the end Wilson
all but threw Trotter out of the Oval Office.

The incident marked one of the great setbacks in the
struggle for racial equality in America, and it revealed Wilson's own attitudes toward black Americans.
Perhaps more important, it revealed a general American
attitude that was not to be substantially changed until
the civil rights movement of the 1950s and 1960s, culminating in the Civil Rights Act of 1964.

Trotter was spokesman for the National Independent
Equal Rights League, a rival to the then fledgling
National Association for the Advancement of Colored
People. He was an M.A. graduate of Harvard, class of
1895, and the first Afro-American member of the honor
society of Phi Beta Kappa. In 1901 he became editor of
The Guardian in Boston and and wrote vigorously against
racism in America. With equal vigor he attacked the
moderation of both Booker T. Washington and the NAACP.
By the turn of the century, the states of the Old
Confederacy had put severe restrictions on black voting, imposing poll taxes, literacy requirements, and
ownership of property as voting qualifications. Booker
T. Washington, founder of Tuskegee Institute, believed
that the franchise was not as important to blacks as
intellectual and economic improvement. He looked forward to some distant future when blacks might regain
the franchise after they had made progress in other ar-

eas. Trotter believed that political action by blacks
was necessary before any other progress was possible.
And political action required blacks to have the vote.[1]

It was an irreconcilable difference. Trotter attacked Washington furiously in the pages of The
Guardian. In 1903 when Washington spoke in Boston,
Trotter and his sister interrupted the speech and were
arrested.[2] Trotter was eventually tried and briefly
jailed for his part in the disruption.[3]

In 1912 Trotter supported Wilson in the presidential
election, which Wilson won only because the Republican
Party was divided. Blacks had been Republican since the
Civil War, when a Republican president, Abraham
Lincoln, issued the Emancipation Proclamation. They did
not take kindly to Wilson, who was both a Democrat and
a Southerner. As Arthur S. Link, Wilson's foremost biographer, points out, blacks had reason to be doubtful
about Wilson. Josephus Daniels, one of Wilson's early
supporters and friends, editor of The Raleigh News and
Observer, wrote in an editorial of October 1, 1912,
that the South voted solidly Democratic out of

> the realization that the subjection of the negro
> [sic], politically, and the separation of the negro,
> socially, are paramount to all other considerations
> in the South short of the preservation of the
> Republic itself. And we shall recognize no emancipa-
> tion, nor shall we proclaim any deliverer, that

---

[1]Stephen R. Fox, The Guardian of Boston: William Monroe
Trotter, New York, Atheneum, 1970, p. 36.

[2]Fox, pp. 50-52.

[3]Fox, p. 57.

falls short of these essentials to the peace and
welfare of our part of the country.[4]

Daniels wrote this editorial in the midst of the
1912 Presidential campaign.

Wilson appealed to blacks to support him, and many
of them--including Trotter--did so. Trotter and Wilson
met with each other in July 1912. They apparently got
on well. Wilson spoke feelingly to various black groups
about his willingness to deal with blacks "fairly and
justly."[5] The statements were equivocal. What is "fair"
or "just" to one person may seem unfair and unjust to
another. Nevertheless, blacks had little choice, and
many supported Wilson. Link points out that Wilson received more black votes than any previous president in
history.[6]

Yet Wilson quickly disappointed black supporters.
When he took office, Trotter asked him not to appoint
Albert Burleson, a Texan, to be Postmaster General.
Burleson had a reputation of hostility to blacks.
Wilson appointed him anyway, and on April 11, 1913,
little over a month after Wilson assumed office,
Burleson told the Cabinet of his intention to segregate
blacks and whites in the Post Office.[7] Wilson seems to
have made no objection.

Trotter had personal reasons to be concerned with
racial discrimination in the Post Office. His father,

---

[4]Quoted in Arthur S. Link, <u>Wilson: The Road to the White
House, Pr</u>inceton, Princeton University Press, 1947, p.
501.

[5]Link, <u>The Road to the White House</u>, p. 502.

[6]Arthur S. Link, <u>Wilson: The New Freedom</u>, Princeton,
Princeton University Press, 1956, pp. 243-244.

[7]Fox, pp. 169-170

James, worked at the post office in Boston. The elder
Trotter resigned his job in 1882 because a white man
was promoted over him.[8] In 1914 Trotter was plainly fu-
rious over what he felt was Wilson's betrayal. In
November 1913 he led a delegation to the White House,
bringing with him a petition with 20,000 signatures
protesting segregation. As he would do in the following
year, Trotter read an "Address." In it he told Wilson
that "Segregation such as barring from the public lavatories and toilets and requiring the use of separate
ones must have a reason. The reason can only be that
the segregated are considered unclean, diseased or in-
decent as to their persons, or inferior beings of a
lower order, or that other employees have a class prejudice which is to be catered to, or indulged."[9]

Trotter pointed out that no other ethnic group was
segregated and that any of them would regard such segregation as an insult. "If separate toilets are provided for Latin, Teutonic, Celtic, Slavic, Semitic and
Celtic Americans, then and then only would African
Americans be assigned to separation without insult and
indignity."[10] Federal employees had worked together
without segregation in the administrations of President
Grover Cleveland, Trotter said. And he recalled that
when an effort was made to segregate federal employees
on racial grounds, Cleveland stopped it.[11]

In 1913, Wilson's response to Trotter was concilia-
tory. He claimed ignorance and promised to investigate.

---

[8]Fox, p. 19.

[9]The Wilson Papers, November 6, 1913, Vol. 28, p. 491.

[10]The Wilson Papers, November 6, 1913, Vol. 28, p. 492.

[11]The Wilson Papers, November 6, 1913, Vol. 28, p. 493.

He assured Trotter that things would be worked out.[12]
John Lorance, a writer for The Boston Daily Advertiser,
reported on December 9 that in consequence of the meet-
ing with Trotter, Wilson was rolling segregation back.
Lorance's article expressed a sense of triumph that
Wilson had championed the cause of equality. Other
Northern papers reflected the same sentiments.[13]

In fact segregation continued. Josephus Daniels was
now Secretary of the Navy. William Gibbs McAdoo of
Georgia by way of Tennessee was Secretary of the
Treasury. Albert Sidney Burleson was Postmaster
General. All these men were close to Wilson; all of
them were uncompromising segregationists.[14]

So when Trotter returned with another "Address" and
another delegation a year later, he was understandably
angry. He felt betrayed, and his "Address" amounted to
an indictment. Although it maintained an icy sort of
courtesy, the fire of outrage burned beneath the surface. He expressed his disappointment in Wilson's
record on race. Wilson had promised to help "Afro-
Americans," Trotter said. Instead segregation was advancing steadily, and Wilson was doing nothing about
it. Trotter recalled the national petition protesting
segregation and presented to the president by black

---

[12]The Wilson Papers, November 6, 1913, Vol. 28, p. 496.

[13]Excerpts from the newspaper articles, including a long
quotation from Lorance, appear in the notes of the Wilson
papers, Vol. 28, pp. 498-500.

[14]In his article in The Boston Daily Advertiser, Lorance
wrote, "The most active segregation has been found under
Sec. McAdoo of the Treasury Department, under Postmaster
General Burleson of the Post Office Department, and under
Sec. Daniels of the Navy Department." See The Wilson Pa-
pers, November 6, 1913, Vol. 28, p. 499.

Americans a year before. Such segregation existed in "working positions, eating tables, dressing rooms, rest rooms, lockers, and especially public toilets."[15]

Wilson had promised to investigate. Trotter pointed out that despite this presidential promise, segregation had gone on and that in fact it had increased. He reeled off a long list of government departments and structures where segregation was enforced. Trotter said that American "citizens of color" realized "that if they can be segregated and thus humiliated by the national government at the national capital the beginning is made for the spread of that persecution and prosecution which makes property and life itself insecure in the South." He pointed out that blacks who had voted for Wilson were now regretting what they had done. "Only two years ago you were heralded as perhaps the second Lincoln, and now the Afro-American leaders who supported you are hounded as false leaders and traitors to their race. What a change segregation has wrought!" The indignity of segregation robbed blacks of their rights of citizenship, Trotter said. "Fellow citizenship means congregation. Segregation destroys fellowship and citizenship. Consider that any passerby on the streets of the national capital, whether he be black or white, can enter and use the public lavatories in government buildings, while citizens of color who do the work of the government are excluded." Trotter and his delegation were there to ask Wilson to "issue an executive order against any and all segregation of government employees because of race and color and to ask whether you will do so."[16]

---

[15]The Wilson Papers, November 12, 1914, Vol. 31, p. 300.
[16]The Wilson Papers, November 12, 1914, Vol. 31, p. 300.

Having presented his "Address," Trotter entered into a spirited dialogue with Wilson. If he expected the president to grant his desire, he was quickly disappointed. The American people rejoiced in the "really extraordinary advances" that blacks had made, Wilson said. "But we are all practical men," the president said. Being "practical" meant that everyone had to recognize that the races could not mix. Segregation was installed to eliminate "the possibility of friction." And Wilson was sure friction would result if blacks and whites mixed. People should be "comfortable," he thought. Segregationists within the government "did not want any white man made uncomfortable by anything that any colored man did, or a colored man made uncomfortable by anything that a white man did in the offices of the government." He was assured, Wilson said, that conditions for blacks and whites were separate but equal. "I haven't had time to look at the conditions myself, but I have again and again said that the thing that would distress me most would be that they should select the colored people of the departments to be given bad light or bad ventilation yet worse than the others, and inferior positions, physically considered." Solving the problems between the races was going to take generations, Wilson said. Blacks and whites were equal in that they both had souls, he said. But there was the matter of economic equality--"whether the Negro can do the same things with equal efficiency. Now, I think they are proving that they can. After they have proved it, a lot of things are going to solve themselves."[17]

_____

[17]The Wilson Papers, November 12, 1914, Vol. 31, pp. 300-303.

8

Trotter asked a question. What did the president think about the humiliation black federal employees had suffered? Wilson claimed not to know of some of the incidents that Trotter mentioned. He suggested that humiliation was all in the mind. "If you take it as a humiliation, which it is not intended as, and sow the seed of that impression all over the country, why the consequences will be very serious. But if you should take it in the spirit in which I have presented it to you, it wouldn't have serious consequences."[18]

Another member of the black delegation, whom the stenographer was unable to identify, protested that whites and blacks had been working together as clerks for fifty years "without distinction and separation based on their race." It was untenable, this person said, to claim that there was any reason to make the separation now. Trotter broke in. Segregation was inevitably a humiliation, he said.

It creates in the minds of others that there is something the matter with us--that we are not their equals, that we are not their brothers, that we are so different that we cannot work at a desk beside them, that we cannot eat at a table beside them, that we cannot go into the dressing room where they go, that we cannot use a locker beside them, that we cannot even go into a public toilet with them.

There was no friction in going to a public toilet, he said. Black government workers had been going to

---

[18]The Wilson Papers, November 12, 1914, Vol. 31, p. 303.

9

public toilets for fifty years. But when the Wilson administration came in, Trotter said, "a drastic segregation was put into effect at once." This segregation was not caused by friction; it was caused by prejudice on the part of the official who put it into operation.[19]

Wilson broke in here, obviously angry. He condemned Trotter's tone. No one had ever spoken to him like that in the White House before, he said. If this organization wished to speak to him again, it had to have another spokesman. "You have spoiled the whole cause for which you came," he told Trotter.[20]

Trotter insisted that he was telling the truth about what blacks in America believed about Wilson and segregation. But Wilson gave not an inch. When Trotter implied that blacks would not vote for Wilson again, Wilson dismissed the threat as "blackmail" and concluded, "You can vote as you please provided I am perfectly sure that I am doing the right thing at the right time." With that Wilson broke off the meeting.[21]

So the conversation ended in failure. The New York Times in a story headlined, "President Resents Negro's Criticism," reported the next day that Wilson would continue the segregation begun during his administration. Trotter expressed his disappointment in the meeting and announced a mass meeting to be held the following Sunday.[22] A number of newspaper editorials in the

---

[19]The Wilson Papers, November 12, 1914, Vol. 31, pp. 304–305.

[20]The Wilson Papers, November 12, 1914, Vol. 31, p. 306.

[21]The Wilson Papers, November 12, 1914, Vol. 31, p. 308.

[22]The summaries of these newspaper stories are presented as footnotes to The Wilson Papers, November 12, 1914, Vol. 31, pp. 308–309.

10

North condemned Wilson's policies. Oswald Garrison Villard, editor of The New York Evening Post wrote, "The Wilson Administration went out of its way to create the issue it now deplores, and cannot see its way clear to admitting its mistake and reverting to the only defensible position of absolute equality in Government Service."[23]

Wilson held his ground and apparently never reconsidered his position. Had Trotter and others investigated Wilson's past utterances on the subject of race, they might never have entertained the expectations that were now so keenly disappointed.

Wilson was a Southerner, born in Staunton, Virginia, in 1856. His father, Joseph Ruggles Wilson, was a Presbyterian minister. Less than a year after young Woodrow (christened Thomas Woodrow Wilson, he was called Tommy in those days) was born, the Wilsons moved to Augusta, Georgia, and it was there that he passed the Civil War. Link says this about Wilson's sense of being Southern:

> In later life Wilson developed a romantic and extravagant love for the South of legend and song. His letters and addresses are full of expressions of deep feeling for the region. He was one historian, for example, who was not apologetic about the South's history. On one occasion he declared that there was "nothing to apologize for in the history of the South--absolutely nothing to apologize for.'"[24]

---

[23]Editorial of November 17, 1914; quoted in a note to The Wilson Papers, Vol. 31, p. 328.

[24]Link, The Road to the White House, p. 2.

That history, of course, included slavery. And Link
says, "He was characteristically a Southerner in his
attitude toward the Negro. Like most Southerners of the
upper class, his tolerance of and kindliness of the
Negro were motivated by a strong paternalistic feeling."[25]

Paternalism and kindliness meant that though Wilson
did not believe in violence toward blacks, he thought
they should be kept in an inferior status until some
unspecified time when they might have earned some
rights to general advancement. Link's "paternalism"
scarcely expresses the extent of Wilson's sense that
blacks did not know what was good for them and had to
be regulated by discreet and wise white men.

Wilson saw blacks in the South as politically incompetent. In an article he tried and failed twice to publish in 1881, Wilson explained the solidity of the old
Confederacy behind the Democratic Party. It was all
caused by the enfranchisement of blacks. Black voting
had been solidly Republican. Southern whites were thus

and an inferior race, or to band themselves in a political union not to be broken till the danger had
passed."[26]

Were blacks born inferior, or were they made inferior by their environment? Wilson is unclear on the
point. He quoted with favor the sentiments of a
Virginian named A. H. H. Stuart who had recently writ-

---

[25]Link, Road to the White House, p. 3.
[26]The Wilson Papers, Vol. 2, pp. 51-52.

ten that Southerners opposed "ignorant sufferage entirely irrespective of race or color. . . . We object to
their votes because their <u>minds</u> are dark,--because they
are ignorant, uneducated, and incompetent to form an
enlightened opinion on any of the public questions
which they may be called on to decide at the polls."[27]
There were, he said in conclusion, some blacks who had
become "extensive land holders and industrious farmers
of their own lands," and these people appeared the
start of "an exceedingly valuable, because steady and
hardy, peasantry."[28]

The South was striving, he thought, to lift blacks
"from degradation."[29] If the Republican Party would accept the situation in the South, the fears of Southern
whites would be mollified. It is difficult to know if
these sentiments represented genuine conviction that
blacks could be uplifted until most of them might have
the vote. His mention of a "steady and hardy peasantry"
may have been an almost subconscious statement of how
far Wilson expected blacks to advance--to a position of
recognizable worth but just as recognizable inferiority. He gave no indication anywhere that he expected
blacks to rise to business or the professions. Certain
it is that he expected blacks to improve themselves
first and only then to be allowed to vote. He expected
this process to require a very long time. Since
progress was under way (he thought) but nowhere

---

[27]<u>The Wilson Papers</u>, Vol. 2, p. 51.
[28]<u>The Wilson Papers</u>, Vol. 2, p. 54.
[29]<u>The Wilson Papers</u>, Vol. 2, p. 54.

near complete, his energies went to restricting black
participation in political life.

These sentiments of the young Wilson did not change.
In his mature work, A History of the American People,
published in five volumes in 1901 and 1902, he discussed the origins of the Ku Klux Klan in the wake of
the Civil War. The Fifteenth Amendment, giving the
freed slaves the right to vote, ensured that "the domi-
nance of the negroes [sic] in the South was to be made
a principle of the very constitution of the Union." It
was a "radical Amendment," said Wilson, and it caused
"the temporary disintegration of southern society and
the utter, apparently the irretrievable, alienation of
the South" from the Republican Party.[30] He says not a
word in support of the notion that blacks required the
right to vote if they were to make good their freedom.

The Klan grew up, he says, around Pulaski,
Tennessee, when young men "finding time hang heavy on
their hands . . . formed a secret club for the mere
pleasure of association."[31] He describes how these young
men rode around at night under the moon, wearing white
masks and with horses sheeted up like ghosts. The aim
of the Klansmen was to frighten blacks. And they succeeded, much to Wilson's evident pleasure.

It was the delightful discovery of the thrill of
awesome fear, the woeful looking for of calamity

---

[30]Woodrow Wilson, A History of the American People, New
York and London, Harper & Brothers, 1901-2, vol. 5, p. 58.
[31]History, Vol. 5, p. 59.

that swept through the countrysides as they moved from place to place upon their silent visitations, coming no man could say whence, going upon no man knew what errand, that put thought of mischief into the minds of the frolicking comrades. It threw the negroes into a very ecstasy of panic to see these sheeted "Ku Klux" move near them in the shrouded night; and their comic fear stimulated the lads who excited it to many an extravagant prank and mummery.[32]

Wilson admits that things went bad when "malicious fellows of the baser sort who did not feel the compulsions of honor and who had private grudges to satisfy" imitated the disguises of honorable Klansmen and did unspecified bad things.[33] It is clear from his account that he thinks that things finally went too far, creating in some places in the South "a reign of terror."[34]

Yet it is also clear from his text that he sympathized with the original aims of the Klansmen even if he did not condone their later, more violent methods. He reports with obvious disapproval an act of Congress of 1871 intended "to crush the Ku Klux Klan and all lawless bands acting after its fashion." Most startling is Wilson's acquiescence in the breaking of the law by white Southerners. It was not their law; therefore, he seems to say, they were not bound by it. White leaders

---

[32]History, Vol. 5, p. 60.

[33]History, Vol. 5, p. 62.

[34]History, p. 64.

in the South were shut off from the ballot, he says. So
they had to act in other ways:

> Those who loved mystery and adventure directed the
> work of the Ku Klux. Those whose tastes and princi-
> ples made such means unpalatable brought their in-
> fluence to bear along every counselor of management
> that promised to thrust the carpetbagger out of of-
> fice and discourage the negro in the use of his
> vote. Congress saw where they meant to regain their
> mastery, at the polls, and by what means, the intim-
> idation and control of the negroes without regard to
> law,--the law thrust upon them, not their own; and
> hastened to set up a new barrier of statute against
> them.[35]

Throughout his discussion of Reconstruction, Wilson
takes what was by his time the canonical Southern view:
Reconstruction was an unmitigated evil thrust upon the
South by the victorious North, and the heart of the
evil was the franchise extended to the former slaves.
He never asks questions that might have helped him and
his readers understand why Reconstruction came about.
The Southern states had been in a state of rebellion
against the authority of the Central government. In
other societies, the leaders of a vanquished rebellion
had usually been shot, hanged, or sometimes publicly
tortured to demonstrate the futility of rebellion. The
defeated Southerners were not treated so cruelly, but
the victorious Washington government did have some reason to put the former secessionist states on probation.

---

[35]History, Vol. 5, pp. 72-74.

Depriving former rebels of the vote was better than depriving them of their lives. But to Wilson the historian, the Republican party in charge of Reconstruction
was dastardly to the core and its measures wicked just
becaused they attempted to make full citizens of blacks
who had so long been in bondage. Since the
Reconstructionist measures were imposed on the South by
force, Southerners had no moral obligation to obey
them.

Although Wilson never quite praises or condones the
violence of Klansmen and others, he does explain it and
excuse it. Clearly, in his view of things, violence was
a lesser evil than black suffrage. He is particularly
indignant at Charles Sumner, the senator from
Massachusetts who had been before the war an abolition-
ist and after the war an advocate of federal support of
black rights in the South. Sumner, says Wilson, insisted that blacks have "social rights" as well as political rights.[36]

What were these "social" rights? They were incorporated in the Act of Congress of February 1875, that
"gave the federal courts the authority, by appropriate
process and penalty, to enforce the right of negroes to
accommodation in public inns, theatres, railway car-
riages, and schools, and to service upon all juries,
upon the same footing as white persons."[37] For Wilson,
"social" rights clearly included any public association of blacks and whites on grounds of apparent

---

[36]History, Vol. 5, p. 97.
[37]History, Vol. 5, p. 98.

equality. In short, Wilson the historian was advocating the segregation of the races not legally ended until the civil rights legislation of the 1960s. The 1875 Act, says Wilson, "For eight years . . . was to fail utterly of accomplishing its object and yet to work its work of irritation, to be set aside at last by the Supreme Court (1883) as an invasion of the legal field of the States which no portion of the constitution, new or old, could be made to sustain."[38] The word irritation seems significant in view of Wilson's later use of the word friction in his discussions with William Monroe Trotter.

Wilson believed that any association of blacks and whites in the workplace, in schools, or on public transportation was bound to create problems. This was the unexamined principle behind all his pronouncements on relations between the races. Therefore, the states, and the federal bureaucracy, could segregate the races. His interview with Trotter in 1914 shows an unwillingness to consider that the humiliation experienced by blacks under such segregation had anything to do with the matter. The humiliation was not intended; Wilson's view was that blacks should accept his own good intentions and make the best of them. Southerners had been entitled to break the law in their wish to enforce segregation; Wilson felt entitled to make rules to the same end.

Most striking in Wilson's History of the American People is how vague it all is. Wilson intended his book for the broad general public. Today, such a writer

---

[38]History, Vol. 5, p. 98.

would tell illustrative anecdotes about people. Wilson almost never tells an anecdote. His statements remain assertions that we are to believe on account of his authority. He gives us little reason to accept that authority. We learn that things were done, but we never learn the mechanism by which they were done. Only now and then does some specific detail break the monotony of tedious assertion. In describing Grover Cleveland, Wilson says, "He was of the open and downright sort that all men who love strength must always relish."[39] He does not tell us that Cleveland had sired a son out of wedlock, a fact well known to the public, a story that might have added some content to the vague adjective downright. In describing the settling of Oklahoma, Wilson comes as close as he ever does to specific occurrence: "At noon on the 22d of April, 1889, at the sound of a bugle blown to mark the hour set by the President's proclamation, the waiting multitude surged madly in, and the Territory was peopled in a single day."[40] The concreteness of that lonely bugle is almost startling in Wilson's interminable catalogs of empty generalizations.

This quality of generality in his writing of history fitted the generalizations he could make about blacks. If his mind had been turned toward the specific, he might have told some stories about responsible, intelligent blacks turned away from the polls by ignorant and violent Southern whites. He might have told stories about victims of the Ku Klux Klan that might have inspired indignation and sympathy not only in readers but

---

[39]History, Vol. 5, p. 171.
[40]History, Vol. 5, p. 212.

in himself. Such stories, had he been interested in
them, might have made him at least relax some of the
rigor of his views. If we know that a specific man in a
specific place has been cruelly denied the vote (no
women, black or white, voted in America at that time),
and if we know all the details of that denial and the
suffering of the would-be voter, we naturally spring to
sympathy with his loss of rights. But Wilson protected
his prejudices by throwing around them a wall of authoritative general statement that made them sound like
virtues, not only to readers but to himself. Individual
blacks did not appear in his pages. Indeed, individuals
scarcely appeared at all except to have their names
called if they were recognized leaders and to have
something general said about them.

It should be said that his prejudices were not
against blacks alone. Wilson's own ancestry was north
European. When he taught at Bryn Mawr and at Princeton,
he offered courses in the history of England and
France. When he came to discuss immigration in the
later nineteenth century, he wrote:

Throughout the century men of the sturdy stocks of
the north of Europe had made up the main strain of
foreign blood which was every year added to the vital working force of the country, or else men of the
Latin-Gallic stocks of France and northern Italy;
but now there came multitudes of men of the lowest
class from the south of Italy and men of the meaner
sort out of Hungary and Poland, men out of the ranks
where there was neither skill nor energy nor any
initiative of quick intelligence; and they came in

numbers which increased from year to year, as if the
countries of the south of Europe were disburdening
themselves of the more sordid and hapless elements
of their population, the men whose standards of life
and of work were such as American workmen had never
dreamed of hitherto."[41]

Wilson's ideas about democracy were built on the assumption that only certain classes and certain people
were worthy of self-government. Arthur S. Link, devoted
as he is to Wilson, discusses this aspect of Wilson's
career with obvious pain. Wilson himself finally admitted to approving of segregation in government departments, claiming that it was "distinctly to the advantage of the colored people themselves."[42] Support for
segregation from the president was bound to have a powerful effect, and to Wilson belongs much of the blame
for the failure of the federal government to support
the black struggle for equal rights until it was forced
to do so by the Supreme Court, the civil rights movement led by the Reverend Martin Luther King, Jr., and
many others, culminating finally in the Civil Rights
Act of 1964.

As Link points out, Wilson was not alone in his
prejudices. Many newspapers and leaders spoke out
against Wilson's segregationist policies. But, says
Link, speaking of Wilson's Cabinet, "If there were any

---

[41]History, Vol. 5, p. 213.
[42]Link, The New Freedom, p. 251.

opponents of segregation in the Cabinet, they did not
then or afterward raise their voices."[43]

Despite the protests against segregation, a majority
of whites in America supported discrimination. The year
after Wilson's last meeting with William Monroe
Trotter, D. W. Griffith brought out his <u>Birth of a
Nation</u>, glorifying the Ku Klux Klan and portraying
blacks as ignorant, malicious, arrogant, and lusting
after white women. The film quoted Woodrow Wilson's
<u>History of the American People</u> to justify the Klan. It
was shown in the White House, though Link holds that
Wilson did not thereby endorse the film. Even so,
Wilson refused to condemn the film publicly. To do so,
he said privately, would be to appear "to be trying to
meet the agitation . . . stirred up by that unspeakable
fellow Tucker."[44] "Tucker" was Trotter; Wilson got his
name wrong. In April 1915, Trotter was charged with as-
sault in Boston when he was refused in his request to
buy a ticket for the film, which he may have intended
to disrupt.[45] Wilson evidently had this incident in
mind, and he could not bring himself to do anything
that might seem to support Trotter's position.

Others were bolder. In May 1915 former President
Charles W. Eliot of Harvard spoke to a mass meeting on
the Boston Common about "Birth of a Nation." He condemned the the "dangerously false doctrine" taught by
the film "that the Ku Klux Klan was on the whole a
righteous and necessary society for the defence of

---

[43]Link, <u>The New Freedom</u>, p. 247.

[44]Link, <u>The New Freedom</u>, p. 253.

[45]<u>Focus on The Birth of a Nation</u>, ed. Fred Silva, Englewood Cliffs, N.J., Prentice-Hall, 1971, pp. 72-73.

Southern white men against black Legislatures led by
Northern white men." Said Eliot, "Undoubtedly, grievous
conditions existed in the South, but they did not jus-
tify the utter lawlessness and atrocities which marked
the trail of the Ku-Klux. There can be no worse teaching, no more mischievous doctrine than this, that lawlessness is justified when necessary."[46]

The philosophy Eliot condemned happened to be the
express view of the president of the United States
about the Klan. Although Wilson did not formally endorse the film, the quotation of his work in the film
itself was an endorsement of the film's fundamental
message. Nothing, not even violent lawlessness, seemed
as bad to Wilson as blacks in control, and surely they
would be in control in many Southern states if they
were given equality with whites.

The popularity of the film was in part testimony to
Griffith's cinematic genius. But the record of the
country at large in civil rights shows that the popularity was also testimony to a racial prejudice of the
American people that was to rule for decades. Woodrow
Wilson's influence on race relations was pernicious.
His meeting with William Monroe Trotter in November
1914 was a disaster for Wilson's long-term reputation,
but more important, it represented a calamity for
blacks, now facing a president who thought he was doing
good. A sadder realization is that Wilson undoubtedly
represented the views of most Americans in his day.
Trotter received vigorous support from a few Northern
papers and liberal groups. None of these counted so
much at the time as the conviction of most American
whites that Woodrow Wilson's prejudices represented
truth.

---

[46]Focus on The Birth of a Nation, p. 73.

Bibliography

Focus on The Birth of a Nation, ed. Fred Silva, Englewood Cliffs, N.J., Prentice-Hall, 1971.

Fox, Stephen R, The Guardian of Boston: William Monroe Trotter, New York, Atheneum, 1970.

Link, Arthur S., Wilson: The New Freedom, Princeton, Princeton University Press, 1956.

Link, Arthur S., Wilson: The Road to the White House, Princeton, Princeton University Press, 1947.

Wilson, Woodrow, A History of the American People, New York and London, Harper & Brothers, 1901-2, vol. 5.

Wilson, Woodrow, The Papers of Woodrow Wilson, ed. Arthur S. Link and other Princeton, Princeton University Press, vol. 2, 1967; vol. 28, 1978; vol. 31, 1979.

24

SOME CONCLUDING NOTES ABOUT THE PAPER

This paper presents primary sources, secondary sources, and the interpretations of the author to arrive at a thesis: President Woodrow Wilson made federal government policy according to his belief that black Americans were inferior to whites. The paper is far more than a mere sticking together of sources. The writer has thought about the material and has arrived at some interpretations that help explain it. He has inferred much from his texts. While Wilson does not say, "I heartily approve of the Ku Klux Klan," he writes about the Klan in such a way that the writer feels justified in inferring that Wilson thought that the Klan was a better choice than giving black Americans the vote.

The author's own point of view is unmistakable: He laments the decisions Wilson made to enforce racial segregation in America. Yet the author does not pour out invective on Wilson's head; the author does not preach to us. A historian can make a judgment on whether certain actions in the past were good or bad; historians do that sort of thing all the time. It is not acceptable in the field of history to preach with vehement emotion either for or against a person or an act in the past. It is sufficient to point out the things Wilson said and the things he did without making vehement denunciations of Wilson himself. Readers can then see that Wilson harmed the cause of equality in America, and they can make up their own minds about his character. We have a right to be angry with Wilson after studying the evidence. Yet anger does no good in the writing of history, and it can irritate readers so much that they stop reading. The reader of this paper does not read it to see how angry the writer is, but to see what Wilson did and why.

The paper moves steadily to develop its thesis. When new information is presented, we are told immediately how that information relates to the thesis of the paper. We are not left wondering. The paper is documented throughout so we can look up the evidence if we want to know more about it. The emphasis on primary sources helps prevent the paper from being a collage of what others have said about Wilson. The thoughtfulness of the author in dealing with his sources is such that at the end we feel we have learned something important from someone who has taken pains to become an authority in this area of Wilson's life and thought.

Answer the questions below by studying the sample paper. Apply these questions to your own writing.

1. What sentence or sentences near the beginning of the paper announce the author's thesis, the main idea that controls this paper?
2. How does the author use quotations? How many block quotations are there in the paper? Why does he use block quotations here and shorter quotations elsewhere?
3. Where does the author use secondary sources? Where does he disagree with his secondary sources?
4. Where does the author make inferences? That is, where does he make plausible suggestions about the meaning of various texts when that meaning is not explicit in the words of the text themselves?
5. Where are the narrative paragraphs in the essay?
6. Where are the expository or interpretative paragraphs in the essay?

7. How can you tell the author's own position on Wilson's views?
8. In what way does the conclusion of the paper mirror some of the ideas in the opening?
9. How would you describe the opening of the paper?
10. How well does the author identify names of people introduced into the paper?

6

Documenting Your Sources

Throughout this book and other books you read about history, you become familiar with documentation—footnotes or endnotes, citations within the text, and bibliographic references. These citations are so common that you take them for granted. You saw them in Dick Curry's paper on Woodrow Wilson; you see them in nearly every book about history that you read. You know by now that historians depend on primary and secondary sources to produce their stories of the past. Indeed, it may be said that to write history is always to write about sources. Other historians want to be able to check the evidence to see if the writer has interpreted it soundly. And historians also use the documentation in books and articles they read to help them in their own research.

It is always good to include in your paper a note on the sources, a description of them, your estimate of how reliable they are, and your sense of how difficult they are to use. This information may appear in a footnote at the beginning of your essay.

Whenever you quote from a source or use information gathered from a source, tell your readers where they can find the quotation or the information. When you quote the exact words of a source, enclose those words with quotation marks or use a block quotation to let readers know where you found them. If you summarize or paraphrase a source, let readers know what you are doing. Otherwise you may be guilty of plagiarism, and plagiarism is the unpardonable sin of the writer.

Here are some simple rules to help you avoid plagiarism and to help you know when to acknowledge that you have taken information from a source.

1. Use a footnote, an endnote, or a mention in your text whenever you quote directly from a source.

A good rule of thumb is to give the attribution for any quotation of three or more successive words. Always put such quotations within quotation marks in the body of your text. Here is a text from a secondary source, Frederick A. Pottle's *James Boswell: The Earlier Years 1740–1769*. Pottle speaks of Samuel Johnson, author of the first great English dictionary and sage of eighteenth-century England:

> Johnson was at this time in his fifty-fourth year, a huge, slovenly, near-sighted scholar, his face scarred by scrofula, his body distorted by compulsive tics, his speech interspersed with absent-minded clucks and mutterings.[1]

You might cite part of this text with a direct quotation followed by a footnote.

When Boswell met him, Johnson was fifty-four years old, "a huge, slovenly, near-sighted scholar, his face scarred by scrofula, his body distorted by compulsive tics, his speech interspersed with absent-minded clucks and mutterings."[1]

Or you can attribute your source in your own text like this:

Frederick A. Pottle says that when Boswell met him, Johnson was fifty-four years old, "a huge, slovenly, near-sighted scholar, his face scarred by scrofula, his body distorted by compulsive tics, his speech interspersed with absent-minded clucks and mutterings."[1]

In some publications—a newspaper story, for example—the format does not allow footnotes or endnotes. Your teacher may ask you to do a short paper without footnotes or endnotes—a brief report, a position paper, a summary of your knowledge on a topic. Even without footnotes and endnotes, you can show in your text that you are quoting someone else's work. You can say, "According to Simon Schama . . . ," or "John Keegan observes that . . . ," or "Western historian Patricia Limerick has said that. . . ."

2. Acknowledge any paraphrase or summary you make of a source.

[1]New York, McGraw-Hill, 1985, p. 113.

Here is a paragraph from the book by Philippe Ariès called *The Hour of Our Death,* a history of attitudes toward death in the Western World:

> Since death is not the end of the loved one, however bitter the grief of the survivor, death is neither ugly nor fearful. On the contrary, death is beautiful, as the dead body is beautiful. Presence at the deathbed in the nineteenth century is more than a customary participation in a social ritual; it is an opportunity to witness a spectacle that is both comforting and exalting. A visit to the house in which someone has died is a little like a visit to a museum. How beautiful he is! In the bedrooms of the most ordinary middle-class Western homes, death has come to coincide with beauty. This is the final stage in an evolution that began very quietly with the beautiful recumbent figures of the Renaissance and continued in the aestheticism of the baroque. But this apotheosis should not blind us to the contradiction it contains, for this death is no longer death; it is an illusion of Art. Death has started to hide. In spite of the apparent publicity that surrounds it in mourning, at the cemetery, in life as well as in art and literature, death is concealing itself under the mask of beauty.[2]

Here is how someone might summarize this passage. The summary would require a footnote or an endnote.

    In the nineteenth century the attitude toward death
    turned into a cult of the beautiful. People gathered
    around the deathbed to participate in what was supposed
    to be an exalting occasion. In fact such rituals were a
    way of hiding death, of granting an artistic illusion
    to the moment of life's end. The thought seemed to be
    that if people could put a beautiful mask on death, it
    would cease to be death.

Since the thought of the paragraph depends on the material in the source, the writer should indicate his or her indebtedness. One might do so with a footnote at the end of the paragraph, but it would be even better to write a statement like this:

[2]Phillippe Ariès, *The Hour of Our Death,* trans. Helen Weaver, New York, Vintage Books, 1982, p. 473.

```
As Phillippe Ariès has said, the attitude toward
death in the nineteenth century turned into a cult of
the beautiful.
```

You could go on then with the paragraph as it was written in the first version, putting a footnote at the end.

3. Acknowledge any important ideas that you have picked up from someone else.

Sometimes you can make this acknowledgment in your text; sometimes you need to add a footnote. You might say something like this:

```
In Richard Lanham's view, The Book of the Courtier,
frequently called an aristocratic book, is in reality a
bourgeois creation.
```

However you do it, let people know where you have got your ideas and where they should go to find further information in your sources.

4. Do not footnote common knowledge or common expressions or allusions.

Common knowledge includes information so widely known that it would seem foolish to note its source. You do not have to give footnotes to the information that Franklin Roosevelt was elected president in 1932 or that the Japanese attacked Pearl Harbor on December 7, 1941, or that Thomas More wrote the book *Utopia* or that Columbus discovered America.

Nor do you have to footnote common expressions. You do not have to tell people that the sentence, "Pride goeth before destruction," comes from the Bible or that "To be or not to be" and "to paint the lily" come from Shakespeare. Sometimes you may not know what constitutes common knowledge in the area of history where you are writing. You can usually decide by looking at several books or articles to see if they contain the information. Innumerable books, for example, will give lists of the popes or of the monarchs of England. Therefore you need not footnote the information that Pope Clement II ruled the Catholic Church from 1046–1047. But the medieval gossip that he was poisoned because he was a German and not an Italian would have to be footnoted to the scholars who have concerned themselves with Clement's life. Sometimes you put notes in parentheses. If you are writing about only one book, as you might be in a thoughtful report about the book, some teachers will ask that you give the full bibliographic information about that book in a special appendix at the back of your paper. Then you can put the page numbers in parentheses.

Ladurie believes that men in medieval Montaillou
were more likely to be able to marry for love than were
women (p. 189). He means that men had choice in the
matter while the women they chose often did not.

In some papers you may use several sources, all fully described in your bibliography. If you do not then wish to use footnotes or endnotes, you may refer to the works by citing their authors.

Medieval women seemed to marry while they were still
adolescents, but young men remained single until they
were twenty-five or even older (Ladurie, p. 262). But
some evidence suggests that the numbers of marriages
fluctuated. People tended to marry with greater frequency in time of plague as if to make up for the population carried off by illness (Braudel, p. 71).

If you cite two or more books by the same author, you may have to add a short title within the parentheses to let readers know that you are quoting from first one book and then the other. Suppose you wished to use Fernand Braudel's books, *The Wheels of Commerce* and *The Structures of Everyday Life*. You might write a paragraph like this with abbreviated titles set within your parenthetical annotation:

Both Columbus and the Vikings learned that the cur-
rents and the winds of the Atlantic ocean will easily
carry ships both East and West (Braudel, Structures p.
409). But for a very long time the largest sea-going
commerce was carried in small ships that traded along
the coastlines of Europe and never ventured far out
into the great and dangerous ocean (Braudel, Wheels p.
362).

Notice that the abbreviated title is underlined or set in italics just as one would set off the full title of the book.

FOOTNOTES AND ENDNOTES

Parenthetical annotation gained in favor among history teachers and publishers for a long time. Such notes are easy to write and inexpensive to set in type. But they are distracting. Computer word processing programs make footnoting simple, and so footnotes and endnotes are regaining their old popularity.

As the names suggest, footnotes are placed at the bottom or foot of the page where the reference to a source is made; endnotes are placed at the end of the paper. The advantage of the footnote is that the reader can look down from the text to the footnote easily. Some readers and editors find footnotes distracting because they break up the flow of the eye across the page. The reader seeing a footnote number feels compelled to glance down to the corresponding note thus breaking the train of thought created by the reading.

Endnotes are less obtrusive. As might be expected, the complaint of some readers against footnotes is reason for others to extol them. In a footnote, the source is immediately available; one does not have to turn to another page to find it, as one does to find an endnote.

Follow the procedure required by your teacher or your publisher. That advice also holds for the forms of the notes, whether they be footnotes or endnotes. Historians have never adopted a standard footnote form such as that used by the Modern Language Association. The main requirements of most teachers and editors are that the notes provide enough information to allow readers to look up the sources for themselves. If your source is a book, provide the name of the author, the title, the place and the year of publication. Most editors and teachers like to have the publishing company listed, too. Books sometimes migrate from publisher to publisher. A first edition may be published by one company, a second edition by another. The publisher of a book in hardcover often sells the rights of the book to another firm to bring out in paperback. Page numbers may change from edition to edition as pages are added or deleted or as the typeface is changed so that the contents of the book take up more or less room. A book may be published by one company in the United States and by another in Great Britain in the same year, and the two editions may be slightly different. Including the name of the publisher in the footnote or endnote will reduce confusion caused by this migration. The publisher's name usually goes between the city where the book is published and the date of publication.

An article in a journal should include the author's name, the title of the article, the date of publication, and the page numbers of the article. Many editors and teachers like to have the volume number of the journal, though others find this information redundant. The February 1988 issue of *The American Historical Review* happens to be Volume 93 of that journal. In a few libraries the volume number might be stamped on the outside of the binding without any additional information about the month and the year, so that in looking at a shelf in a dimly lit library stacks, you might find Volume 93 more easily than you might locate "February 1988." In my experience the year of the volume is stamped on the spine of most bound periodicals in nearly all libraries. To my mind the volume number in a bibliographical reference is an unnecessary complication. But again, consult your teacher or your editor, and follow directions.

Some Examples

Following are some sample footnotes or endnotes for various kinds of publication. I prefer the simple method of setting off every part of the note with commas and using a period at the end, and no publisher of mine has ever objected. Note that the number at the beginning of the note is slightly elevated in this style—an elevation easily performed by word-processing programs and computers these days. I use the abbreviation "p." for "page" because it clearly sets off the page number from other data in the entry. Some editors and teachers omit it, especially after parentheses.

[1]David McCullough, <u>Mornings on Horseback</u>, New York, Simon and Schuster, 1982, p. 183.

It is probably somewhat more common to place the publication data within parentheses:

[1]David McCullough, <u>Mornings on Horseback</u> (New York, Simon and Schuster, 1982), p. 183.

or

¹David McCullough, <u>Mornings on Horseback</u> (New York, 1982), 183.

Many publishing houses omit the name of the publisher of books listed in footnotes and bibliographies. It is unlikely, for example, that two publishing houses in New York City would have issued David McCullough's *Mornings on Horseback* in the same year. The place of publication is therefore enough to locate the edition of the book that you have used. In the footnote or endnote, the first name of the author is given first. In the bibliographic note, which we will come to in a minute, the last name of the author is given first.

A book that has been translated into English from another language usually has the translator's name after the title:

²Jacob Burckhardt, <u>The Civilization of the Renaissance in Italy</u>, trans. S. G. C. Middlemore, Greenwich (Conn.), Phaidon Publishers, 1965, p. 14.

or

²Jacob Burckhardt, <u>The Civilization of the Renaissance in Italy</u>, trans. S. G. C. Middlemore, (Greenwich [Conn.], Phaidon Publishers, 1965), 14.

Note that the place of publication, "Greenwich," has the abbreviation of Connecticut after it to show that the book was not published in Greenwich, England.

A book with several authors lists them in the order they appear in the book itself.

Joseph R. Strayer and Hans W. Gatzke, <u>The Mainstream of Civilization</u>, 4th ed., San Diego, Harcourt Brace Jovanovich, 1984, p. 146.

or

Joseph R. Strayer and Hans W. Gatzke, <u>The Mainstream of Civilization</u>, 4th ed., (San Diego, Harcourt Brace Jovanovich 1984), 146.

Note that the edition number in this citation appears after the title. Books often go through several editions. You need not give an edition number for the first edition; you should make reference to the number of later editions.

A work in more than one volume may be cited in several different ways:

```
Jaroslav Pelikan, The Christian Tradition, vol. 4,
Reformation of Church and Dogma 1300-1700, Chicago and
London, University of Chicago Press, 1984, p. 155.
```

or

```
Jaroslav Pelikan, The Christian Tradition, vol. 4,
Reformation of Church and Dogma 1300-1700,1 (Chicago
and London, University of Chicago Press, 1984), 155.
```

This work is the fourth volume in a series called *The Christian Tradition*. Volume 4 has its own title. Many writers would omit the series title *The Christian Tradition* and give only the title of Volume 4 as though it were an independent book. Anyone looking in a card catalog under the name "Pelikan, Jaroslav" would find the title easily even without the series name.

Some books are collections of essays, and you may wish to cite only one essay in the group. Give the author of the essay you wish to mention, put the title of the essay in quotation marks, and give the title of the book, the editor of the book, the publication data, and the page number.

```
³J. H. Baker, "Law and Legal Institutions," William
  Shakespeare, ed. John F. Andrews, New York, Charles
  Scribner's Sons, 1985, Vol. 1, p. 43.
```

An article in a standard reference work is cited without page or volume numbers, though the title of the article is placed within quotation marks. It is assumed that those looking for the article will know to look it up in the alphabetic order that such articles appear in such works. The year of the edition does appear in the note because articles are revised from edition to edition.

```
"Charles V," Encyclopaedia Britannica, 1974.
```

An article in a scholarly journal may be cited in one of the two following ways. The first is without the volume number of the periodical:

```
⁴Natalie Zemon Davis, "History's Two Bodies," The
American Historical Review, February 1988, p. 6.
```

The other method of citation uses the volume number and places the date within parentheses:

```
⁴Natalie Zemon Davis, "History's Two Bodies," The
American Historical Review, 93 (February 1988), 6.
```

In citing a book review, you give both the author of the review and the title and the author of the book being reviewed. In your citation of the review, you do not have to give the publication data of the book that is reviewed.

```
⁵Elizabeth G. Gleason, review of Venetian Humanism
in an Age of Patrician Dominance by Margaret L. King,
The Sixteenth Century Journal, 18 (Winter 1987), 611.
```

Often, as in the paper on Woodrow Wilson and segregation, you may use a footnote or endnote to add information that you do not wish to place in the body of your paper. You may add bibliographic material to that information, or you may let the information stand by itself.

You may cite manuscript materials as simply as possible. For example, if you use letters, you can give the writer, the person to whom the letter was sent, and the date.

```
⁶Jones to Smith, September 3, 1873.
```

When you cite a book or an article for the second time, you need put only the author's name and the page number. Readers will assume that you are referrring to the same work that you have previously footnoted.

```
⁷Davis, p. 10.
```

If you have used several books by the same author, you may devise a short title that refers to the book you intend to cite in an additional reference to the work.

```
⁸Braudel, Wheels, p. 140.
```

In multivolume works you can sometimes use the volume numbers with an abbreviation of the work. *The Yale Edition of the*

Complete Works of St. Thomas More is usually abbreviated *CW.* A paper that cited many works of More scattered throughout the volumes of the edition might use this abbreviation like this, especially for notes after the first reference to the work:

⁹More, <u>CW 8</u>, p. 731.

Note that both the abbreviation and the volume number are usually placed in italics or underlined.

BIBLIOGRAPHIES

The bibliography, an alphabetical listing by author of works cited in your paper, is placed at the end of your work. You have seen the bibliography for the paper on Woodrow Wilson and segregation. If the author is not given, the work is alphabetized according to the first word of the title. Just as variations appear in the style of footnotes and endnotes, so do they also appear in bibliographies. Some editors and teachers require periods to be placed to set off the author from the title and the title from the publication data.

Breen, Quirinus. <u>John Calvin: A Study in French</u>
  <u>Humanism</u>. Chicago, 1931.

Or, you could make the bibliographic reference like this:

Breen, Quirinus, <u>John Calvin: A Study in French</u>
  <u>Humanism</u>, Chicago, University of Chicago Press, 1931.

Note that in both instances, the body of the review is indented under the first line. This style allows readers to spot the author's name quickly, and on a page it clearly sets off each bibliographic entry. Notice, too, that in both styles of making a bibliographical entry, the parentheses around the publication data are omitted.

Here are some sample bibliographic entries.

For a book with more than one author, the last name of the first author is placed first, and the other names are left in their natural order.

Strayer, Joseph R, and Hans W. Gatzke. <u>The Mainstream</u>
  <u>of Civilization</u>, 4th ed. San Diego, Harcourt
  Brace Jovanovich, 1984.

or

Strayer, Joseph R, and Hans W. Gatzke. <u>The Mainstream
    of Civilization</u>, 4th ed. San Diego, Harcourt Brace
    Jovanovich, 1984.

For a multivolume work:

Skinner, Quentin, <u>The Foundations of Modern Political
    Thought</u>, in two volumes, Cambridge (Eng.), Cambridge
    University Press, 1978.

<u>Commonwealth History of Massachusetts</u>, in five volumes,
    ed. Albert Bushnell Hart, New York, The States
    History Company, 1927, 1928.

Note that this entry of a set of essays composed by many different authors begins with the title and puts the editor after the title.
    For an article from a journal:

Savage, Gail L. "Friend to the Workers: Social Policy
    at the Ministry of Agriculture Between the Wars."
    <u>Albion</u>, 19 (Summer 1987), pp. 193–208.

Note that for articles, you give the page numbers in the periodical
where the article is found. This will help your colleagues find the article easily.
    For an article from a collection of essays:

Baker, J. H., "Law and Legal Institutions," <u>William
    Shakespeare</u>, ed. John F. Andrews, New York, Charles
    Scribner's Sons, <u>1</u>, 1985, pp. 41–54.

Note that this article appears in the first volume of a three-volume
set. The italicized or underlined <u>1</u> indicates volume 1. You might have
placed the abbreviation <u>vol.</u> before the <u>1</u>.

7

Suggestions about Style

"Style" in writing varies from writer to writer, and general agreement on style is hard to come by. Some historians are vivid and dramatic. Others are content to be more prosaic. As I have already pointed out on several occasions, honest historians never make up details for the sake of drama. The best advice is to write clearly enough so readers can understand your work without having you there to explain it to them.

Most writers work hard all their lives to develop a style they find both natural and attractive, one that others can understand and enjoy. No writer ever finds a style that pleases everybody. You do best to begin forming your own style by making it as readable as you can, trying at the same time to avoid monotony of expression.

We know a lot about readability—the qualities of a style that can be read without undue confusion. Specialists in rhetoric have done research about what makes a text reasonably clear. Some of this research has been incorporated into computer programs designed to measure the readability of various texts. Readability and style are not identical. Few books are clearer than the primers used to teach children how to read in the first grade, but such a style becomes quickly tedious to adult readers. A good style combines readability and elegance. The following suggestions take much of this research on readability into account. Keep them in mind as you write. They are not carved in granite, and you can violate them now and then, but if you violate them too often, the readability of your work will suffer.

1. Write in coherent paragraphs.

Paragraphs are groups of sentences bound together by a controlling idea. You have been reading paragraphs throughout this book, taking them for granted because they are common to nearly all the prose we read. Paragraphs help readability. Indentations break the monotony of long columns of type. They help readers follow the text with greater ease, providing special help when we lift our eyes from the page and then must find our place again. They signal a slight change in subject from what has gone before. They announce that the paragraph to follow will develop a thought that can usually be summarized in a simple statement.

Paragraphs vary considerably in length. Newspaper and magazine paragraphs are much shorter than paragraphs in books. There are no firm rules about paragraph length. The paragraph was not defined until the second half of the nineteenth century; those who did the defining could not agree on length, and the disagreement persists today. Long paragraphs can become disorganized, and even a well-organized long paragraph may create eye strain. Short paragraphs may give an appearance of choppiness, of shifting from subject to subject without giving readers time to adjust. A good rule of thumb is to have one or two indentations on every typed manuscript page. It is only a rule of thumb—not a divine command.

The first sentence in any paragraph shows the direction the paragraph will take. Here is a paragraph by William Manchester, who in this part of a book on recent American history describes various political figures who became popular immediately after World War II.

Joe McCarthy, late of the Marine Corps, was reelected circuit judge in 1945. He immediately began laying plans to stump his state in the following year under the slogan "Wisconsin Needs a Tail Gunner in the Senate," telling voters of the hell he had gone through in the Pacific. In reality McCarthy's war had been chairborne. As intelligence officer for Scout Bombing Squadron 235, he had sat at a desk interviewing fliers who had returned from missions. His only wartime injury, a broken leg, was incurred when he fell down a ladder during a party on a seaplane tender. Home now, he was telling crowds of harrowing nights in trenches and dugouts writing letters to the families of boys who had been slain in battle under his leadership, vowing that he would keep faith with the fallen martyrs by cleaning up the political mess at home—the mess that had made "my boys" feel "sick at heart." Sometimes he limped on the leg he broke. Sometimes he forgot and limped on the other leg.[1]

[1]William Manchester, *The Glory and the Dream,* Boston, Little, Brown, 1973, p. 394.

The first sentence of this paragraph, *Joe McCarthy, late of the Marine Corps, was reelected circuit judge in 1945,* sets the topic—Joe McCarthy, later Senator from Wisconsin who gained worldwide notoriety (some would say infamy) for his reckless charges that communists had infiltrated government, universities, and even churches in America. The second sentence picks the main thought of the first sentence by using the pronoun *he* and by telling us something else about McCarthy. The third sentence continues the subject by telling us about "McCarthy's war"—and so through the paragraph. We could summarize this paragraph by saying, "Here is a collection of facts about the political rise of Joseph McCarthy after World War II."

In any paragraph you can draw lines between connectors, words like the pronoun *he* in the paragraph about McCarthy repeated throughout the paragraph. Sometimes the connector will be a word in one sentence that is repeated in the next sentence. The connectors are important because they tie together your sentences—and therefore your thoughts. They help keep your ideas and information in an orderly framework. You can often test paragraph coherence by seeing if every sentence has a connector word that joins its thought in some way to the previous sentence all the way back to the first sentence in the paragraph.

The structure of paragraphs is usually either serial or listing. In the serial pattern of paragraph development, the second sentence will develop a word or thought in the first sentence, the third sentence will develop a word or thought in the second sentence, the fourth sentence will develop a word or thought in the third sentence, and so on to the end. In the list pattern, sentences in the paragraph make in essence an interchangeable list of items that support the general statement made in the first sentence.

In the serial paragraph, the order of the sentences cannot be rearranged because each sentence depends on the one immediately before it. In the list paragraph, the order can be rearranged after the first sentence because the sentences that come afterwards all have an equal relation to that first sentence. Here are three short paragraphs that illustrate these principles. The first two are serial paragraphs. The third paragraph is a listing paragraph, beginning with a general sentence that is then supported by sentences relatively independent of each other. The other sentences are a list that help expand the first sentence. The paragraphs are about the assassination of Ngo Dinh Diem, dictator of South Vietnam, killed by his own troops in

November 1963 during the Vietnam War. The first two paragraphs are straight narratives; the third is an explanation.

> At Saint Francis Xavier, a French mission church in Saigon's Chinese district of Cholon, the early morning Mass had just celebrated All Souls' Day, the day of the dead. A few minutes later, the congregation gone, two men in dark gray suits walked quickly through the shaded courtyard and entered the church. South Vietnam's President Ngo Dinh Diem and his brother Nhu, haggard after a sleepless night, were fugitives in the capital they had once commanded.
>
> A few hours earlier, rebel soldiers had crushed the last of their loyal guards. The remote church was their final haven. They prayed and took Communion, their ultimate sacrament. Soon their crumpled corpses would be sprawled ignominiously across the deck of an armored car that rumbled through the streets of Saigon as the people cheered their downfall.
>
> Diem, though dedicated, was doomed by his inflexible pride and the unbridled ambitions of his family. Ruling like an ancient emperor, he could not deal effectively with either the mounting Communist threat to his regime or the opposition of South Vietnam's turbulent factions alienated by his autocracy. His generals—some greedy for power, others antagonized by his style—turned against him. His end, after eight years in office, came amid a tangle of intrigue and violence as improbable as the most imaginative of melodramas.[2]

The order of sentences in the first two paragraphs cannot be changed. That is a characteristic of serial paragraphs. Because each sentence depends for its meaning on the sentence that comes immediately before it, you cannot change the sentences around without changing their wording. But the order of sentences in the third paragraph could be changed after the first sentence. Every sentence in the last paragraph reaches back to the first sentence with its controlling word "Diem." You could write the paragraph like this:

```
Diem, though dedicated, was doomed by his inflexible
pride and the unbridled ambitions of his family. His
end, after eight years in office, came amid a tangle of
intrigue and violence as improbable as the most imagi-
```

[2]Stanley Karnow, *Vietnam: A History,* New York, Penguin, 1984, p. 277.

native of melodramas. His generals--some greedy for
power, others antagonized by his style--turned against
him. Ruling like an ancient emperor, he could not deal
effectively with either the mounting Communist threat
to his regime or the opposition of South Vietnam's tur-
bulent factions alienated by his autocracy.

The simplest and most readable paragraphs are like these two models, the serial paragraph and the listing paragraph. They are the two fundamental structures of the English paragraph. Now and then the two structures are combined in a single paragraph. The first sentence contains a word or words that are repeated in the next sentence. Words or thoughts in that second sentence are repeated in the third sentence. But then the fourth sentence—or a later sentence—may go back not to the sentence immediately before it but to the first sentence in the paragraph. The following paragraph shows a mixed character. Some of its sentences cannot be rearranged because they pick up ideas in the sentences immediately before them. Some of them can be rearranged because they look back beyond the previous sentence to an earlier thought. The paragraph deals with Greek colonization around the Mediterranean Sea in classical times:

South Italy and Sicily became known as Magna Graecia—Great Greece. By the sixth and fifth centuries the cities of this area were larger, wealthier and more populous than those of mainland Greece. The Greeks who settled there became the *nouveaux riches.* Everything they built was "bigger and better." Their temples were larger and more ornate. Culturally, however, they lagged behind mainland Greece. Like colonial Americans, they were anxious for "civilization" from the homeland. They imported creative men of all sorts, from artists to poets and philosophers, from Pindar, who wrote victory odes for the tyrant of Syracuse, to Plato, who tried to establish his ideal state under a philosopher king in Sicily. They regularly sent competitors in splendor to the Olympic Games, and if its contestants were victorious the entire city rejoiced in celebration. When a certain Exaenetus of Acragas was a victor in the ninety-second Olympiad, he was conducted into the city in a procession consisting of three hundred chariots, each drawn by two white horses. Two stories, though probably apocryphal, well portray how ravenous the Sicilian Greeks were for culture. In 413 BC survivors of the catastrophic Athenian campaign against Syracuse were given aid and shelter by the hostile Sicilian population in return for recitations of the verses of the playwright Euripides. Another story tells of a Caunian ship fleeing from pirates which once tried to sail into Syracuse but was forbidden entry until the sailors recited songs from Euripides.[3]

The repetition of the word "they" or "their" in sentences 4 through 9 hold the paragraph together. The tenth sentence, beginning "When a certain Exaenetus," supports the statements made in the previous sentences about the pride of the Sicilian Greeks. The next sentence builds on that idea. The last two sentences develop thoughts in that sentence, the one beginning "Two stories." The sentences that tell the stories could be easily transposed as long as the word "another" was used to introduce the second story. The paragraph is a combination of serial methods and list methods of writing a paragraph. A paragraph like this one on the Sicilian Greeks is readable because the word "Greeks" and pronouns referring to "Greeks" are repeated throughout. Although it does not strictly conform to one of the two patterns I have noted, it does follow the pattern of repetition that holds all good paragraphs together. Every sentence in the paragraph recalls a sentence in an earlier part of the essay; at the same time, every sentence adds a piece of new information and anticipates a sentence yet to come.

These patterns of repetition hold all prose together. They make nonfiction writing recursive. That is, it continually looks back on itself, providing help to the short-term memory so that the reader is continually reminded in various subtle ways of the thesis of the essay, of where the essay has been and of where it is going. Every sentence after the first in an essay refers both to something that has come before it and to something that comes after it. Some word (or words) in every sentence picks up a thought from a previous sentence and some word (or words) in every sentence points to something that follows in a later sentence. The paragraph is a convenient way of joining sentences in a visual unity, but each sentence within the paragraph is connected by the picking up of some idea from a previous sentence and then expressing some idea that can be picked up by the next sentence.

[3]Robert J. Littman, *The Greek Experiment: Imperialism and Social Conflict, 800–400 BC*, New York, Harcourt Brace Jovanovich, 1974, pp. 47–49.

Narrative paragraphs—paragraphs that relate events happening one after another—seldom have a topic sentence. Even without the topic sentence, they, like expository paragraphs, develop unity by repetition. They connect one sentence to the next by some sort of repetition of words or ideas. Here is a paragraph from Wallace Stegner's book *The Gathering of Zion,* his story of the Mormon trail and the travel of Brigham Young's early group of Mormon immigrants to Utah. The "Revenue Cutter" in the paragraph is the name of a small boat the Mormons found operating on the river when they arrived at the crossing. Stegner calls the Mormons "saints" because that is what they called themselves.

Travelers late in the season often found the North Platte here clear and shrunken and shallow enough to be waded, but in June it was a hundred yards wide and fifteen feet deep, with a current strong enough to roll a swimming horse. (It did in fact drown Myers' buffalo horse.) The Revenue Cutter could carry the wagons' loads, but the wagons themselves were a problem. While some of the saints brought down poles from the mountain and worked at making rafts, others experimented with swinging wagons across the river on a long rope tied to the opposite bank. Two wagons tied together keeled over on striking the far shore, breaking the reach of one and the bows of the other. Four lashed together proved to be stabler, but too heavy to handle. One alone, with an outrigger of poles to steady it, was caught by the current and the strong southwest wind and rolled over and over. The best system appeared to be ferrying one at a time on a clumsy raft. A backbreaking day of that, up to their armpits in icy water, and they had crossed only twenty-three wagons. It rained and hailed on them, and the wind blew. The river was rising so fast they were afraid of being held up for days; and thinking of themselves, they also thought of the great company crowded with women and children who would soon follow them. Brigham put a crew to hewing two long dugout canoes from cottonwood logs and planking them over to make a solid ferryboat.[4]

The internal connections of this paragraph are made of the repetition of words having to do with the river, the wagons, and the people. Were there a topic sentence to this paragraph, it would be something like this: "These were the problems the Mormons had in getting

[4]Wallace Stegner, *The Gathering of Zion,* New York, McGraw-Hill, 1964, p. 148.

their wagons across the North Platte River." Such a sentence is not necessary because the action, built sentence by sentence by a careful pattern of repetition, is clearly understandable.

Although narrative paragraphs seldom have topic sentences, analytical paragraphs usually do have them. Analytical paragraphs explain information. We explain documents or people or events by paying attention to those details that make up a text, a personality, or a happening. We look at the relation of those details to one another. We try to see how they came about. We see what they contribute to the whole. A general statement at the beginning of an analytical paragraph usually states the issue that is going to be explained. Here is a paragraph from a recent article in *The American Historical Review* on attitudes toward property at the time of the American Revolution. The author, James L. Huston, argues that the Americans who shaped our democracy did not believe in concentrations of wealth but thought that property should be distributed fairly evenly through the population. Here is the third paragraph of Huston's article:

> The revolutionaries' concern over the distribution of wealth was prompted by a tenet in the broad and vague political philosophy of republicanism. In contrast to nations in which monarchs and aristocrats dominated the state, republics embodied the ideal of equality among citizens in political affairs, the equality taking the form of citizen participation in the election of officials who formulated the laws. Drawing largely on the work of seventeenth-century republican theorist James Harrington, Americans believed that if property were concentrated in the hand of a few in a republic, those few would use their wealth to control other citizens, seize political power, and warp the republic into an oligarchy. Thus to avoid descent into despotism or oligarchy, republics had to possess an equitable distribution of wealth.[5]

Huston provides a general statement in his first sentence. The rest of the paragraph explains and develops the thought in that first sentence.

When you are explaining an idea or an event in history, you will often help readers see where you are going if you present a general-

[5]James L. Huston, "The American Revolutionaries, the Political Economy of Aristocracy, and the American Concept of the Distribution of Wealth, 1765–1900," *The American Historical Review*, October 1993, p. 1080.

ization in the first sentence and develop that thought through the rest of the paragraph. Such sentences help readers understand the information in the body of the paragraph. Without such general statements, clearly expressed and carefully related to the following sentences, readers can easily lose the thread of an explanation, become frustrated, and refuse to continue reading.

Such sentences help especially in paragraphs where you answer the question "Why?" Why did something happen? Why did someone write this text? Why did people believe what they did at the time you are writing about? Topic sentences are also helpful in paragraphs that explain the meaning of ideas or events. Here are three consecutive paragraphs that each begin with a general statement, a topic sentence that introduces an explanation or an answer to various questions that might begin with "Why?"

One of the great blows to American scholarship took place on February 1, 1770, when a modest upland plantation burned to the ground. At the time, it was an entirely personal tragedy. The young master of Shadwell, Thomas Jefferson, was absent, and his mother was with him, so no lives were lost. But time would reveal what the world had lost: It had lost a world. Except for a few papers he carried with him—his account book, mainly, and two books of his private "florilegia"—this compulsive writer and record keeper lost everything he had composed to the age of twenty-seven, along with the library he had been assembling with great care and cost for over a decade.

The loss is easily put in concrete terms. Though the great Boyd edition of Jefferson's papers promises to stretch out to the crack of doom, only twenty-five pages of the first volume are devoted to his writings before the fire occurred—letters saved by their recipients (mainly John Page), one advertisement in the newspapers, one draft of a public paper.

That accident goes far toward explaining one of the odd things about Jeffersonian scholarship. Despite the fact that the Declaration of Independence is Jefferson's most influential composition, studies of his intellectual world tend to pick him up after 1776, when he wrote it. Daniel Boorstin, for instance, tries to reconstruct the "lost world" of Jefferson's thought around the Philadelphia activities of the American Philosophical Society, which Jefferson did not even join until 1780, and where he was not active for another decade—not, that is, until his Philadelphia years as Secretary of State and Vice President, the years when he turned fifty.[6]

The author here carefully leads us step by step through an explanation, giving us the subject of each paragraph by making a generalization at the start. Then he supports that general statement with details supplied by successive sentences. As he was writing, he probably organized his own thoughts and directed the flow of his prose by using those generalizations. You will find that writing a good general sentence at the beginning of a paragraph will help you think of the details to support it. A clear general statement at the beginning of a paragraph will also help you eliminate interesting but distracting details irrelevant to the general statement.

2. Illustrate your major generalizations by specific references to evidence.

Evidence is any supporting information that helps readers believe any general statement you make. If you try to prove that people in the sixteenth century were unusually fearful, mention the horrifying representations of death in art, the hundreds and hundreds of fearsome paintings of the last judgment, the predictions of the end of the world, the cult of magic and astrology, and the common fear of ghosts and other apparitions. Give the sources of this information. Be detailed enough to help your readers believe you know what you are talking about.

If you say that Woodrow Wilson had racist ideas, quote from his works to demonstrate them. A series of flat generalizations or assertions following one on the other may seduce the writer into believing that he has proved a case when in fact he has only stated a case that must yet be proved.

The following paragraph contains a general statement—that death rates in the seventeenth century were so high that survivors tended to marry several times. We have the general statement at the beginning of the paragraph (a typical topic sentence), followed immediately by some confirming evidence. Peter Laslett, the author of the book from which this paragraph is taken, has compiled the raw data

[6]Gary Wills, *Inventing America: Jefferson's Declaration of Independence,* Garden City, N.Y., Doubleday, 1978, pp. 167–168.

for his conclusions by studying the parish records of English churches, the books in which church officials kept records of births, marriages, and deaths. Some town records kept rough census figures that also became a part of his book.

> The heavier mortality of that age made for more frequent re-marriage. Records of the number of times people had been married unfortunately only rarely survive, but it so happens that the listing of the people of Clayworth in 1688 was carried out with such care that this information can be worked out from it. There were at that date 72 husbands in the village, and no less than 21 are recorded as having been married more than once: 13 of them had been married twice, 1 a number of times unspecified, 3 three times, 3 four times and 1 five times. Of the 72 wives, 9 had been previously married; 1 of the 7 widowers and 1 of the 21 widows are known to have been married more than once. This is spectacular confirmation for one single community of a law which seems to obtain for the whole pre-industrial world, that once a man reached the marriage age he would tend to go on getting married whenever he found himself without a wife. At Adel in Yorkshire one old man married his sixth wife in 1698 and his seventh in 1702. The law holds for women too, but is weaker in their case, because widows found it more difficult to get husbands than widowers to get wives. Together with the much marrying majority of the older people there may also have been a small community of persons who did not marry at all.[7]

You may sometimes quote statistical information to establish a point made by the first sentence in a paragraph. Be sure your statistics are reliable and that you provide the source, and be sure that you use statistics responsibly.

3. To test the coherence of your papers, see if the first and the last paragraphs have some obvious relations.

In most published writing, the first and the last paragraphs of a book, a chapter in a book, or an article have such coherence that you can read them without reading the intervening material and have a fairly good idea of what comes between. Now and then you will find a piece of writing where the first and last paragraphs do not have a clear

[7]Peter Laslett, *The World We Have Lost,* New York, Charles Scribner's Sons, 1971, p. 104.

relation. Writers wishing to be sure that their work does hold together can help their efforts by seeing to it that each of their papers ends in a paragraph that reflects some of the words and thoughts appearing in the first.

Try to avoid the easiest way of achieving this harmony between first and last paragraphs. That is, don't start with a summary of what the paper will be about and then conclude with a summary of what it has been about: "In this paper I am going to examine the controversy over General James Longstreet's actions at the battle of Gettysburg"; "In this paper I have examined the controversy over General James Longstreet's actions at the battle of Gettysburg." Such beginnings and endings are tedious, and all readers, including your teachers, expect essays that come after such introductions to be boring.

Here are the first and last paragraphs of an essay on the education of England's unfortunate King Edward V, the 12 year-old child who, with his younger brother the little Duke of York, was pushed aside by Richard III in 1483 and later vanished. It has generally been assumed that Richard had him killed, though a few vehement "Ricardians" still maintain Richard's innocence. Study the repetitions in the final paragraph of key words and thoughts expressed in the first paragraph and see how they suggest a binding together of the essay, a coherence that makes reading easier and more comprehensible. The first paragraph:

> The childhood and education of Edward V necessarily make up the whole of his biography, for he was only twelve when he was overthrown as king in 1483 and died, almost certainly, before he was thirteen. They are also worth studying, however, because of the careful and well-recorded arrangements which were made by his father, Edward IV, for bringing him up. The education of previous heirs to the English throne, of course, had been careful, too. Special households were organized for them to live in; nurses, mistresses and masters were assigned to care for them and teach them; and they were trained in a wide range of knowledge, skills and activities. The education of Edward V conformed to this tradition, but seems to have differed in being more deliberately and formally planned in advance. Written ordinances were drawn up to regulate the prince's education in 1473 when he was nearly three, and reissued ten years later with appropriate revisions as he entered upon his adolescence. It is in the formulation of these ordinances, where hitherto princely education had been mainly informal, that the particular interest of Edward's

childhood lies. The article which follows is centered on discussing them and placing them in context.[8]

The last paragraph:

> The arrangements of Edward IV for his son look paradoxical today. They brought an almost unprecedented formality to the prince's education, yet they allowed him to become too closely associated with a single group of important, yet unpopular men. This had not been true of the upbringing of earlier royal princes, to nearly such an extent. Their household officers had usually been lesser men uninvolved in high politics, or respected men holding equable relationships with the royal uncles and other great magnates. Henry VII, in the bringing up of his own two sons, was to revert to this older less dangerous tradition. In the case of Edward V, his close association with the Wydevilles and the Greys proved disastrous. Their unpopularity stimulated and enabled Richard III to seize and remove them from power, and then left Edward V as a defenceless remnant of their party. Richard could hardly feel safe after robbing Edward of men so close to him, and to whom he was probably sincerely attached: the removal of Rivers and Grey must have helped to dictate the elimination of Edward. Sadly, the education which was intended to build him into a great king became, instead, a principal element of his downfall.[9]

You can see the relation of these two paragraphs through their repetition of thoughts about Edward V's education. The word "education" is repeated, and thoughts about it are expressed in both paragraphs.

Sometimes the connections between the first and the last paragraph are subtle. Sometimes they are clear. But we can believe from seeing the mirroring of these two paragraphs that the article presents a coherent statement of his case. You can help coherence by seeing to it that some thought expressed in the first paragraph has a valid conclusion in the last. If you can see no connection between your first and your last paragraphs, you may do well to check your essay to see if indeed it develops one major thesis throughout. You may have gone

[8]Nicholas Orme, "The Education of Edward V," *Bulletin of the Institute of Historical Research,* November 1984, p. 119.

[9]Orme, p. 125.

off the track into a digression so that your essay does not hold together.

4. Begin most sentences with the subject.

Sentences are statements about subjects. In published American English, about three-fourths to four-fifths of the sentences and independent clauses within sentences begin with the subject. This principle is often undermined by well-meaning writing teachers who tell their students to vary sentences by inverting them—that is, by putting the verb before the subject. Alternatively, they tell students to begin with a participle or to do something else to keep the subject from coming first. Yet any examination of published English in widely read books and articles will show the proportion of openings with the subject that I have mentioned here. This is the pattern that rhetorician Francis Christensen discovered years ago.[10] Only about one-fourth or one-fifth of sentences by almost any American writer begin with something other than the subject; these other beginnings or "openers" are usually some sort of adverb—a word, phrase, or clause. A few sentences begin with conjunctions. Now and then a sentence begins with a participle or a participial phrase, but most sentences begin with the subject. You will help keep your thinking clear if in writing sentences you think first of the subject, then of what you want to say about it.

The main point of this advice is to say that our natural way of composing sentences, whether we speak or write, is to name a subject and then to make a statement about it. Sometimes inexperienced writers are paralyzed by the thought that they begin too many sentences with the subject. They feel a laudable desire to vary their sentences and try to change the beginnings. They often then write amazingly complex and difficult sentences that are a strain to them and their readers. Let nature take its course: Begin most of your sentences with the subject.

This suggestion is more important than it may seem at first. Many sentences go astray and become hopelessly confused because the writer does not know clearly what he wants to say. He (assuming the

<hr/>

[10]Francis Christensen and Bonnijean Christensen, *Notes Towards a New Rhetoric*, 2nd ed., New York, Harper and Row, 1978, pp. 61–73.

writer is male) puts words down, hoping for some sort of inspiration, and he keeps writing without any order, winding and winding until at last he comes on the period like a man struggling to save himself from drowning.

Be sure that you write each sentence to make a clear statement about a subject. Don't bury your real subject, the most important element in the sentence, in a dependent clause. Indeed, most readable writers use dependent clauses only once or twice in every three or four sentences. The main action of your sentence should be in the main clause, and in that clause you should identify the subject as the most important element about which a statement is to be made.

Here is a paragraph that demonstrates the common English and American practice of beginning most sentences with the subject. It is from a book by an English scholar on social life in France under King Louis XIV. The subjects are in italics.

> *We* have examined in some detail the three kinds of surgeons practicing in France 300 years ago. *We* must not, however, overlook the surgeon-dentists, who in some ways were an even cruder body of technicians. *Charlatans and quacks* abounded in dentistry, since its practitioners were quite prepared at any time to turn their hand to a dozen related trades. *Some progress towards modern techniques* was, of course, being made at this time. About the middle of the long reign *it* became possible to secure a set of dentures, which, though almost useless for eating, at least filled up the gaps when the wearers went into polite society; and *we* read of the fair Mademoiselle de Gournay who removed her upper set before a meal, but restored them to their proper place when conversation demanded. On the whole, however, *we* must pity the unfortunate victims of Grand-Siècle dentistry, who were often bled for toothache. Indeed, *it* is with no surprise that we read that, like the king, some preferred to treat themselves with cotton wool soaked in oil of cloves, whilst others resorted to the old wives' method of stuffing the cavity with a mixture of earthworms and wax.[11]

Four of these sentences begin with the subject. Three begin with various kinds of adverbs—two prepositional phrases acting as adverbs

---

[11]John Laurence Carr, *Life in France Under Louis XIV*, New York, G. P. Putnam's Sons, 1970, pp. 83–84.

and one with a simple adverb, *indeed.* Here it is easy to see the tendency of a readable writer to place the subject either at the very beginning of the sentence or shortly thereafter, following some sort of fairly simple adverbial construction.

Always consider the subject as the linchpin of your sentence. Everything revolves around it. It should be simple and clearly stated. It should also come at the beginning of the sentence most of the time. When you do not begin with the subject, usually begin with some sort of adverb, either a word or a phrase.

> *Although efforts to assert unity of purpose through governments or through state-created corporations failed,* many Americans hoped that the republic would enable them to act as one, just as they could worship together though affiliated with no single denomination.[12]

The sentence in italics is an adverbial clause.

You may use adverbial prepositional phrases to begin a sentence to answer the questions *where, why,* and *how.*

You may also begin some sentences with a conjunction. Some sentences may be inverted. That is, the verb may come before the subject: "Gone forever was the dream of a united Europe under a French Empire." Don't begin many sentences with participial openings. They can be confusing.

```
Looking for gold and silver in ancient tombs, most
nineteenth-century archaeologists were hardly more than
grave robbers.
```

The participial opening is *Looking for gold and silver in ancient tombs.* Such an opening must modify the subject of the sentence, and this one correctly modifies the subject *archaeologists.* But it is easy to go astray with such openings:

```
Digging up graves for treasure, we can see now that
the nineteenth-century archaeologists were hardly more
than grave robbers.
```

---

[12]Oscar and Lilian Handlin, *Liberty in Expansion: 1760–1850,* New York, Harper and Row, 1989, p. 221.

Here the participial opening modifies the subject, but the meaning of the sentence is now distorted. Did we dig up the graves for treasure? That is what the sentence says. Readers speeding along in that text will have to stop and hesitate a moment before deciding that you have made a mistake. Such pauses are irritating.

If you must use a participial opening, make it modify the subject it should modify in the sentence. The wrong word used as a subject will confuse readers momentarily even if by application they can discover your meaning. You should never create needless work for your readers.

Good writers much more commonly begin most of their sentences with the subject but change the predicates to add variety. The next several points in this list will help you change your predicates.

5. Keep subjects as close to their verbs as possible.

The most readable writers seldom interrupt the natural flow of their sentences by placing a dependent clause after the subject. Like the general principle that most sentences begin with the subject, this is another you can verify by reading almost any popular (and therefore readable) prose. It is not absolute. Every writer sometimes puts a word or a phrase or even a clause between a subject and a verb. But take care not to overdo it. Here is a fine, readable paragraph by historians Oscar and Lilian Handlin:

> The healing image meant much to a government, not all of whose statesmen were pure of heart and noble of impulse. On January 30, 1798, the House of Representatives being in session in Philadelphia, Mr. Rufus Griswold of Connecticut alluded to a story that Mr. Matthew Lyon of Vermont during the war had been forced to wear a wooden sword for cowardice in the field. Thereupon Mr. Lyon spat in Mr. Griswold's face. Sometime later, Mr. Griswold went to Macalister's store on Chestnut Street and bought the biggest hickory stick available. He proceeded to the House, where, in the presence of the whole Congress and with Mr. Speaker urging him on, he beat Mr. Lyon about the head and shoulders. An effort to censure both actors in the drama failed. [13]

[13] Oscar and Lilian Handlin, p. 160.

Note how many subjects and verbs in the sentences of this paragraph are unseparated by other words.

6. Use an occasional rhetorical question.

The rhetorical question is one that you, the writer, ask so that you may define a problem you wish to pursue or an issue that seems pertinent to your discussion. You ask the the question to answer it yourself. Sometimes you ask the question to show readers how obvious your answer is. Here is the English historian Charles Ross writing about Richard III and the death of the little princes in the Tower in 1483. Having recounted many incidents in which English kings and noblemen had been murdered in the century previous to Richard III, Ross asks a rhetorical question:

> Why, then, should it be supposed that Richard, as king, would depart from this established pattern of *raison d'état,* especially given that his position was more insecure than that of his predecessors, and the legality of his claim seems to have been generally disbelieved?[14]

Notice the way that Rebecca West uses the rhetorical question to make a point about the French at the turn of this century.

> Meanwhile the French had endured the Franco-Prussian War of 1870–71 and come out of it fairly well because the Germans had been unable to handle the large monetary penalty they had exacted from the defeated nation and had let it disorganize their finances. But the French were now faced with the prospect of another war with Germany. How did they spend the time given them to put their house in order? More foolishly than anybody could have supposed.[15]

7. Use an occasional metaphor or a simile to make a vivid statement.

Metaphors and similes appeal to some familiar experience or perception to illustrate an experience that may not be so familiar. Here is

---

[14]Charles Ross, *Richard III,* Berkeley and Los Angeles, University of California Press, 1983, p. 99.

[15]Rebecca West, *1900,* New York, Viking, 1982, p. 94.

Civil War historian Shelby Foote, speaking of the danger sharpshooting snipers posed to troops in the line, even during lulls in the fighting:

> Because of them, rations and ammunition had to be lugged forward along shallow parallels that followed a roundabout zigzag course and wore a man down to feeling like some unholy cross between a pack mule and a snake."[16]

The simile, "like some unholy cross between a pack mule and a snake," vividly expresses the discomfort of the men Foote is describing.

The comparison of real people to characters in literature often becomes a simile in the writing of history. Here is a passage from Frank Brady's *James Boswell: The Later Years,* in which he compares, by a simile, Margaret Caroline Rudd with Becky Sharp, a self-seeking and manipulating character in William Makepeace Thackeray's nineteenth-century novel *Vanity Fair.* "Mrs. Rudd was the feminine sensation of the year. Like Becky Sharp, she had to make her own way in the world and, like Becky, she was not fastidious about the means she used."[17]

Sometimes metaphors can be expressed by a single word. Arthur Schlesinger, Jr., writes, "As Michigan banks closed, an infection of panic began to spread across the country."[18] Calling the panic an "infection" is a metaphor conveying the idea that the panic was like a disease, spreading relentlessly.

Such metaphors and similes enliven writing. Don't carry them to excess. Used discreetly, they can be a great help.

Avoid clichés, the tired old expressions that we have heard again and again. The essence of the cliché is its predictability. When we hear the beginning of the expression, we know what the end will be. We know that a bolt is always from the blue, though we seldom think that the person who speaks of the bolt from the blue is speaking of

---

[16]Shelby Foote, *The Civil War: A Narrative,* New York, Random House, 1974, vol. 3, p. 297.

[17]Frank Brady, *James Boswell: The Later Years,* New York, McGraw-Hill, 1984, p. 133.

[18]Arthur M. Schlesinger, Jr., *The Crisis of the Old Order,* Boston, Houghton Mifflin, 1956, p. 476.

lightning striking on a clear day. We have heard the expression so often that we think only that it is supposed to indicate a surprising happening. We know that unpleasant facts are often "cold, hard facts" and that people who are foiled by their own manipulations are "hoisted by their own petard," though we do not know why unpleasant truth should be cold and hard, and we have no idea what a petard is. The expression begins and ends without requiring any thought from us or from our readers.

But the fear of clichés should not make us shun occasional figurative language.

8. Avoid the passive voice whenever possible.

In sentences using the passive voice, the verb acts on the subject. In the active voice, the subject acts through the verb. Here is a sentence in the active voice:

```
John F. Kennedy made the decision to invade Cuba.
```

Here is a sentence in the passive voice:

```
The decision was made to invade Cuba.
```

You see at once the problem of the passive voice: It often hides the actor in the sentence. In the active voice, we know who made the decision. In the passive voice, we do not know who made the decision unless we add the somewhat clumsy prepositional phrase *by John F. Kennedy* which makes the sentence read like this: "The decision was made by John F. Kennedy to invade Cuba."

Readable historians seldom use the passive voice. Here is David McCullough, writing about young Theodore Roosevelt's work in the New York state legislature shortly after the deaths of his first wife and his mother. The only passive verb is in italics.

Now week after week, on into March and April, he did little but work, shunting back and forth from Albany to his hearings by night trains. He reported a flood of bills out of his City Affairs Committee—seven, nine, fourteen a day. His outpouring of work, of words printed and spoken, of speeches delivered, of witnesses grilled, of interviews, of inspection tours (of conditions at New York's infamous Ludlow Street jail), of headlong, concentrated energy was utterly phenomenal, surpassing anything he had ever done before and causing those close at hand to wonder how much longer he could maintain a hold on himself. One day in March he reported fifteen bills out of committee, then six more at a night session, and even then his work for the day had only begun. Dissatisfied with a report on his hearings that *had been drafted* by counsel for the committee, he wrote out an entirely new version at a single sitting, working through until morning.[19]

Use the passive if the subject is acted upon and is much more important than the actor. In the following excerpt, the use of the passive is in italics. Historian Eli Sagan is discussing the practice of human sacrifice in the South Seas in times gone by. His focus is on the victims when he uses the passive. The agent in making the sacrifices has been identified already as the tribe itself, acting through representatives chosen by the chief. So here the passive is justified because it keeps the focus on the victims:

> Buganda had a class system based upon differences in wealth and political power, but *there was no pariah class set aside* for unusual contempt, nor was there a certain group of people *from whom human sacrifices were chosen,* as was the case in Mangaia. On Tahiti the victims were war captives kept alive for that purpose, or people of political importance who had become anathema to the ruling powers, or anyone from the lowest class, called *manahune.* Once a Tahitian *victim had been taken* from a particular family, *the members of that family were marked* to end their lives in the same manner. *When ritual homicide was called for,* such people fled and hid themselves until the drum announced *that a suitable man had been taken.*[20]

When you do not have such a clear reason for the passive, use the active voice. We usually want to know who does things, and the active tells us.

9. Keep sentences short enough to be manageable.

Sometimes writers lose control of their sentences and end with long, involved coils of words. Long sentences can be difficult. They

[19]David McCullough, *Mornings on Horseback,* New York, Simon and Schuster, 1982, p. 285.

[20]Eli Sagan, *At the Dawn of Tyranny,* New York, Knopf, 1985, p. 125.

slow readers down and hide your meaning. They may make you lose the thread of your thought. They can be hard to tie into other sentences.

Always keep in mind the most important statement you want to make in every sentence. That is the statement that can be connected to a previous sentence and joined to a sentence you have yet to write. Don't entangle that statement with other information that you cannot develop or that is not a development of some previous information.

One way to keep sentences manageable is to avoid multiplying dependent clauses. Dependent clauses act as adjectives or adverbs and modify other elements in a sentence. In the following paragraph, the dependent clauses are in italics. The paragraph describes the opening of the battle of Manila Bay in 1898 when the American fleet defeated the Spanish navy. (The *Olympia* and the *Baltimore*, also italicized, were American warships.)

> The squadron was now within a mile or so of the city's waterfront, *which lay almost directly to the west.* Shortly after five o'clock, *as the growing early light revealed more of the coastline,* a lookout sighted ships about five miles to the south, *where a hook of land protruded into the bay.* Calkins swung around and thumbed the knob on his binoculars, bringing Sangley Point and the Cavite naval station into sharp focus. A line of gray and white vessels stretched eastward from the point. Above them flew the flame-colored flags of Spain. Dewey turned and spoke an order to the *Olympia's* commander, Captain Charles Gridley. The flagship swung to starboard. The *Baltimore* following astern did the same, and in a few moments the six warships of the squadron were bearing south, the distant Spanish fleet on their starboard bows. The pulse of the warships quickened *as their speed was increased to eight knots.*[21]

The entire paragraph contains four dependent clauses in nine sentences. Only one sentence contains two dependent clauses; none contains three. Six sentences contain no dependent clauses at all.

Writing cannot be reduced to a numerical formula. The ratio of dependent clauses to sentences will vary from writer to writer. Some writers use more, some fewer. If you think your writing is stiff and dif-

---

[21]G. J. A. O'Toole, *The Spanish War: An American Epic 1898,* New York and London, Norton, 1984, p. 183.

ficult to follow, count the dependent clauses in your sentences. You may be able to make your writing more readable by devising ways to reduce the number of such clauses.

10. Don't overuse adjectives.

Adjectives modify nouns; that is, they change the meaning of the noun somewhat. They can also weaken nouns. A good adjective, well used in a necessary place, can brighten a sentence and help readers see the action better. Too many adjectives thicken and slow down the flow of prose. If you use few adjectives, you leave the action of your sentences where it ought to be—in the verbs and nouns.

Study the adjectives in the following paragraph and consider the number of adjectives in proportion to the number of other words:

As the year 1587 drew to a close, a shudder of apprehension ran across *western* Europe. In part it was perfectly *rational* apprehension. As the closing in of winter made it less and less *likely* that the fleet gathering at Lisbon would sail before the year's end, it became increasingly *certain* that come spring it would sail—against England. In fact, although Philip still wrote to his ambassadors that the Armada's destination must remain a secret closely kept, although at Paris Mendoza maintained an *enigmatic* silence, meanwhile trying every *security* and *counter-espionage* device he could think of, although Parma attempted misdirection by putting it about that the *obvious* aim at England was only a blind for a *sudden* descent on Walcheren, the shape of Philip's plan was becoming *unmistakable*. Lisbon was always *full* of foreigners and the least *experienced* observer could tell that this *vast* mobilization of ships and seamen, soldiers and cannon was not meant just to protect the commerce of the Indies or stir up trouble in Ireland.[22]

There are thirteen adjectives in this paragraph, a ratio of about one adjective to every thirteen words. Notice that Mattingly does not pile up adjectives before nouns. He uses many adjective complements, adding to the description of the subject by placing an adjective modifying the subject after the verb.

The proportion of one adjective to every twelve or thirteen words is fairly constant among published writers in history or in any other discipline in America. Like everything else in this list, the proportion is not absolute. Some writers may use more and some may use fewer.

[22]Garrett Mattingly, *The Armada*, Boston, Houghton Mifflin, 1959, p. 172.

But if you think of that ratio and count your own use of adjectives relative to the other words in your writing, you may have some reason to check your prose and to work at reducing the number of adjectives.

11. Don't write long strings of prepositional phrases in your sentences.

Prepositional phrases allow nouns to be used in sentences in an adjectival or adverbial sense. We say, "I can drive home *through Lexington*" to give an adverbial sense of where we can go driving home. We cannot say, "I can drive home Lexingtonly." We say, "The nation required encouragement by its leader." We cannot say idiomatically, "The nation required leader encouragement."

Too many prepositional phrases in a sentence can be distracting. Now and then we will all write sentences with three or even four prepositional phrases. Do not write *every* sentence like that. You will blunt your meaning. See how hard this sentence is to follow:

```
The prohibition movement of the nineteenth century
among liberals and progressives in the large cities and
in the midwest and among certain church groups was part
of a reform sentiment directed against immigrants with
strange ways in contradiction to the values of
Protestants in a rural America.
```

12. Write about the past in the past tense.

Often inexperienced writers striving for dramatic effect will shift into the historical present. They will write something like this:

```
The issue as Calvin Coolidge sees it is this: The
government has been intervening too much in private af-
fairs. He is now the head of the government. He will do
as little as possible. He takes long naps in the after-
noon. He keeps silent when people come to ask him fa-
vors. He says things like this: "The chief business of
the American people is business." He means that any-
thing contrary to business interests is bad. Within a
year after Coolidge leaves office, we have the Great
Depression.
```

Such writing quickly becomes tedious because it is unnatural. In English, we use the past tense in talking about past events.

13. Use the present tense in referring to the contents of writing or art.

A piece of writing or a work of art is always assumed to be present to the person who reads it or observes it. Therefore, you can use the present tense when you report its content unless you are talking about it in a historical context.

```
The Fourteenth Amendment to the Constitution gives
to the citizens of the various states all the rights
guaranteed under the Constitution itself.
    In Moby Dick, Melville portrays an obsessive madness
in Captain Ahab.
```

But sometimes it may be better to use the past tense. This is especially true when you do not intend to give an extended summary of the work.

```
    In his "Cross of Gold" speech delivered at the
Democratic National Convention in 1896, William
Jennings Bryan took the side of impoverished farmers
who thought that inflation would help raise the prices
they received for their crops.
```

CONCLUSION

If you think about these stylistic devices, you may begin looking more closely at the writing you enjoy to see the forms writers use to keep you moving through their texts. Learning to read is part of learning to write. You learn to read and write best not by consulting a book of grammar and syntax but by noticing carefully the devices good writers use to woo readers.

8

Conventions

Historians make up a broad community; like most communities they have their conventions, their ways of doing things. The conventions are not laws; people are not arrested and put in jail for violating them. Even so, members of the community notice when conventions are violated—just as they notice when someone blows her nose on a linen table napkin at a formal dinner or wears a tuxedo to a football game. As a writer you want to woo your readers—to make them respect you, believe your evidence, and accept your point of view. It's a good idea to follow the conventions followed by other members of the group you are trying to influence.

All of us follow conventions in every community to which we belong. The conventions of historians are not unlike others. The conventions of going to the theater, for example, are violated when someone in the audience decides to play the harmonica while on stage Hamlet is delivering his soliloquy on whether it is better to be or not to be. The conventions of weddings are violated if the father of the bride starts selling popcorn to the audience as the minister is about to pronounce the vows. The conventions of courtesy are violated if when we are introduced to a perfect stranger we suddenly howl with laughter and tell him that he is the ugliest person we have ever seen—even if he is.

Conventions may not be logical, but they are necessary. They provide expectations that help people to get along with each other, to understand each other, and to work together. The conventions of historians allow them to communicate with each other and with other interested readers. If you habitually violate the conventions, you run the risk of not being taken seriously. Your readers may even turn hostile because you frustrate the expectations they have built up from years of reading. It makes no sense to irritate them in that way.

Irritate them with new and radical views if you have the evidence, but don't irritate them out of carelessness.

MANUSCRIPT CONVENTIONS

Most writers and most students nowadays use computers with word processing programs. Take advantage of the marvelous ability of the computer to generate clean copy. You can set the format of a computer to fit any manuscript style required by your teacher. You can mark up a printed copy of your work, then write the corrections onto your disk, and print out a clean copy. Computers make things much easier for writers and readers alike; use them when you can.

The appearance of a manuscript tells readers many things about the writer. Readers can look at a manuscript and tell what the writer thinks of them. A slovenly, scarcely legible manuscript is a sign that the writer cares little for the subject or the readers. The writer may care deeply—just as the parent who screams at children may love them. Still it is not pleasant for children to be screamed at, and it is not pleasant for readers to be forced to read an almost illegible paper.

The presentation of your paper in some respects resembles the presentation of food in a fine restaurant. You would be irritated if your waiter in an expensive restaurant served the main course on a plate that he snatched out of a pile of dirty dishes, wiped off with his apron, and banged down on the table in front of you. A sloppy paper can irritate the readers who should enjoy it.

Formats vary. Your teacher may give you a format to follow. Lacking instructions from your teacher you will not go wrong if you follow the format of the model research paper on Woodrow Wilson in Chapter 5 of this book. Here are some generally accepted conventions.

1. Use $8\frac{1}{2}$ by 11-inch white bond paper. Twenty-pound bond is best. It is heavy enough to handle easily and to make a nice contrast with the type or the ink you use. Hard-pressed teachers reading three dozen research papers appreciate such favors. Do not turn in your final draft on flimsy colored paper.
2. Write on one side of the page only, and leave margins wide enough for comments your teacher may wish to make. If you type or use a

computer, always double-space. Use a fresh ribbon. A faded ribbon makes typewriter print difficult to read; a faded ribbon on a computer-driven dot-matrix printer makes the words almost illegible. If you submit a handwritten copy, use lined white paper and write, in dark blue or black ink, on every other line. Do *not* use red, green, purple, or brown ink. Besides looking tacky, such inks tire your reader's eyes.

3. Use a cover page for your papers. On it place the title, your name, the name of your teacher, the name of your course, and the time your class meets. Teachers who grade a lot of papers sometimes get them mixed up on their desks. You will help your hard-working teacher immeasurably if you make it easy for him or her to place your work.

4. Number your pages. When you do not number your pages, you make your paper difficult to comment on and almost impossible to discuss in class. Sometimes teachers copy papers to distribute to the class, and sometimes papers fall on the floor and the pages are scattered. Numbering pages is one of the basic conventions of writing that have been around since the beginning. Every word processing program numbers pages, usually in the menu for "layout" or "format." Don't be lazy. Find the steps your program uses to number pages, and use them; be professional.

5. Fasten the pages of your paper with a paper clip or with a staple in the upper left-hand corner. Stiff binders are a nuisance to the instructor, adding bulk and making it awkward to write comments in the margins. Don't use them.

6. *Always* make a second copy of your paper, either by photocopying it or by printing out a backup from your computer. Papers do get lost, computers break down, or we make mistakes and erase our work. Always make a second copy just in case something happens to the original. If you use a computer, make a backup disk with a copy of your essay on it.

Corrections in the Final Copy

You should revise your paper enough to catch most casual errors—typos, misspellings, words left out, words duplicated, and so on. Even so, you may find a few others just as you are ready to hand the paper in, or you may want to change a word or two here and there at the last moment. Carefully write these corrections in, using black ink. Be sure your changes are neat and legible.

THE USE OF QUOTATIONS

You will frequently quote from both primary and secondary sources. These quotations (Don't call them "quotes") will give authority and style to your papers. Here are some things to remember.

1. Always use the American system of quotation marks. The primary American quotation mark is made with two apostrophes set together like this:

   `"History is the essence of innumerable biogra-`
   `phies," Thomas Carlyle said.`

   Quotations within quotations are set off with single apostrophes like this:

   `Bingham declared, "I entirely reject Carlyle's`
   `statement that 'History is the essence of innu-`
   `merable biographies' because history is both`
   `more and less than biography."`

2. Periods and commas used at the end of a quotation always go within the quotation marks.

   `"We learn from history that we learn nothing`
   `from history," Hegel said.`
   `Voltaire said, "The history of the great events`
   `of this world is scarcely more than the history`
   `of crimes."`

3. A comma, a colon, or a semicolon used before a quotation to introduce it is placed before the first quotation marks.

   `Thomas Jefferson said this: "Blest is that na-`
   `tion whose silent course of happiness furnishes`
   `nothing for history to say."`

   `In worrying about predestination, Thomas Aquinas`
   `said, "Man has free choice, or otherwise coun-`
   `sels, exhortations, commands, prohibitions, re-`
   `wards and punishments would be in vain."`

Mrs. Carter H. Harrison, wife of a former mayor
of Chicago, denounced the film Birth of a Nation
in unambiguous terms; "It is the most awful
thing I have seen."

4. A question mark at the end of a quotation goes within the final quotation marks if the quotation itself is a question; it goes outside the final quotation marks if the quotation is not a question but is being used within a question.

   Question mark that is part of the quotation:

Professor Buttram posed this question: "Why was
a blatantly racist movie such as Birth of a
Nation so popular?"

   Question mark not part of the quotation:

What did Francis Hackett, writing of the
Reverend Thomas Dixon in the March 20, 1915, New
Republic, mean when he said, "So far as I can
judge from this film, as well as from my recol-
lection of Mr. Dixon's books, his is the sort of
disposition that foments a great deal of the
trouble in civilization"?

5. Semicolons and colons always go outside the final quotation marks setting off a quotation:

"He is yellow because he recklessly distorts
Negro crimes, gives them a disproportionate
place in life, and colors them dishonestly to
inflame the ignorant and the credulous"; such
was the judgment of Francis Hackett of The New
Republic on the "yellow journalism" of the
Reverend Thomas Dixon, author of the book made
into the movie Birth of a Nation.

"I am tired of being dependent on men I despise
from the bottom of my heart": So spoke General
George B. McClellan, commander of the Union Army
of the Potomac in July 1862 when he was angry
and disgusted with Abraham Lincoln and his
Secretary of War, Edward M. Stanton.

6. It is nearly always better to use shorter quotations than longer ones. You can often incorporate a phrase or a clause from a source and give the flavor and the information you want to convey.

Bruce Catton called the battle between the iron-
clad ships <u>Monitor</u> and <u>Merrimack</u> a "strange
fight," for, as he said, "Neither ship could really hurt the other."

7. Always be sure that you incorporate quoted material into your writing so that the grammar and syntax are correct.

Don't do this:

"The major spiritual autobiographies in
English," says Jerome Buckley, has some of the
qualities of an account of a religious conversion experience.

But do this:

"The major spiritual autobiographies in
English," says Jerome Buckley, have some of the
qualities of stories of religious conversion.

8. For any quotation longer than four or five lines, indent the entire quotation five spaces and set it up as a block within your text. Double-space the block quotation, and do not enclose it with quotation marks. Some teachers prefer that block quotations be single-spaced. Ask your teacher about that preference. In preparing manuscript for print, block quotation should always be double-spaced to make life easier for hard-working typesetters—and also to ensure

fewer typographical errors. Since double-spacing of block quotations is an accepted standard in publishing, you should use it in your papers—unless your teacher objects.

Use quotation marks for any quoted material within the block quotation. General practice places a colon at the end of the sentence that introduces the block quotation, but this practice is not always observed. Here is an example of a block quotation appearing after an introductory sentence by the writer of a paper:

Robert Caro's biography of Lyndon Johnson is unrelenting in its account of how many people who knew Johnson as a college student disliked him. But Johnson had power with the administration. Caro tells the story of what happened when the student newspaper at the University of Texas at San Marcos was about to run an editorial that criticized Johnson:

> Sometime during that term--the month cannot be determined--Star editor Mylton Kennedy wrote an editorial satirizing Lyndon Johnson's "relationships with the faculty" and with President Evans. But the editorial never appeared--because, Kennedy says, Johnson "went to Dean Speck." The newspaper had been set in type, and the presses at the Buckner Print Shop were just beginning to roll, when over their rumble, Kennedy heard the telephone ring. When Kennedy answered it, Speck was at the other end. "Have you got an editorial in this issue about Lyndon Johnson?" he asked. And when Kennedy admitted that he did, the dean shouted, "Stop the presses!" (Those were literally the words Speck used, Kennedy says.) He demanded that Kennedy bring him the editorial. And after he read it, he ordered Kennedy to remove it from the paper and confiscated the few copies already in print.[1]

---

[1] Robert A. Caro, *The Years of Lyndon Johnson: The Path to Power*, New York, Knopf, 1982, p. 197.

9. Use ellipsis marks to indicate words you leave out between the quotation marks with which you enclose quoted material. To make ellipsis marks, write three periods, placing a space between each period and whatever comes before and after it. Ellipsis marks . . . are made like this. Notice that there is a space between the word *marks* and the first period that comes after it, a space between that period and the next, a space between the second period and the third, and a space between the third period and the word *are.*

Here is an example:

Original source:

```
The Rosenbergs were not, prior to their arrest
anyway, prominent national figures.
```

Quotation with some words left out indicated by ellipsis marks:

```
In his history of political murder, Franklin L.
Ford says of the Rosenbergs, executed for spying
in the summer of 1953, "The Rosenbergs were not
. . . prominent national figures."
```

Do not use ellipsis marks at the beginning of a quotation. Some writers and editors have taken to beginning quotations with ellipsis marks to indicate that the quotation does not include all of a text. But the quotation marks themselves indicate that part of a text is being separated from its context.

What not to do:

```
Rebecca West says that the Archduke Franz
Ferdinand of Austria Hungary ". . . was a superb
shot, and that is certainly a fine thing for a
man to be, proof that he is a good animal, quick
in eye and hand and hardy under weather. But of
his gift Franz Ferdinand made a murderous use."²
```

²Rebecca West, *Black Lamb and Grey Falcon,* New York, Penguin Books, 1984 (first printed 1941), p. 334.

10. Change capital letters to lowercase or lowercase letters to capitals in quoted material when your purpose is to make the quotation fit into your own sentence. Suppose that you wish to quote this sentence from Richard Ellmann's biography *James Joyce,* where Ellmann comments on the city of Trieste in 1920 when, in consequence of World War I, it has passed from Austrian to Italian rule:

> Under Austria the city had been full of ships; now its harbor was almost deserted.

Here would be one way to use the quotation:

```
Ellmann, writing of Joyce's return to Trieste in
1920, says that "under Austria the city had been
full of ships; now its harbor was almost de-
serted."
```

Do not use brackets to indicate that you have changed the capitalization of the *u* in *under.* Do not do this:

```
Ellmann, writing of Joyce's return to Trieste in
1920, says that "[u]nder Austria the city had
been full of ships; now its harbor was almost
deserted.
```

The practice has taken hold among some editors of putting brackets around a letter that has been changed from capital to lowercase or from lowercase to capital in a quotation. The practice distracts us from reading, and you should not do it.

OTHER CONVENTIONS ABOUT MECHANICS AND GRAMMAR

Most people feel anxious about grammar, supposing they do not know it well and imagining that they make mistakes all the time. In fact most of us know grammar well enough to use it reasonably well. We learn grammar from our families and others with whom we regularly speak, and we know it well enough to communicate. Written language is more formal than spoken language, and writing is much more difficult than speaking. Sometimes in the physical labor of writing our minds wander, and we make errors; that is, we violate conventions. Most people can spot their errors in grammar by reading their work aloud. You can usually trust your ear. When something you have written doesn't sound right, check it out in an English handbook or ask a friend. (Writers collaborate all the time in real life; they should do so in school, too.) The grammar we use in writing is set by editors and writers themselves. It has not changed much in the last century. You encounter it in your textbooks, magazines, daily newspapers, and your own writing. It is a part of mass literacy—the general expectation in the modern world that most people can read. Mass production of any sort requires standardization, and mass literacy has brought about a certain standardization and simplification of grammar. By following the standards, you increase the ease by which readers follow your work. The following are some sources of common difficulties that come up in writing papers. The list does not represent a complete summary of English grammar. If you have other problems, buy a good English handbook and study those areas that give you the most difficulty.

1. Form the possessive correctly. The possessive shows ownership or a particular relation. We speak of John's pen or Prizzi's honor. In both, the apostrophe and a final -s form the possessive. Here are some examples:

> Jane's computer
>
> Mike's house
>
> Napoleon's plan
>
> Lee's family
>
> Churchill's policy

Some writers and editors will add only an apostrophe to singular nouns ending in -s. Thus, the possessive may be Erasmus' works, Chambers' book. But the preferred practice is to make the possessive of these words in the same way that we make the possessive of other singular nouns.

> Erasmus's works
>
> Chambers's book

For plural nouns that end in -s, add the apostrophe to form the possessive.

the Germans' plan
the writers' consensus
the neighbors' opinion
the philosophers' view

Plurals that do not end in *-s* form the possessive like singular nouns.

women's history
men's fashions
children's rights

The possessive pronouns used before the thing possessed are *my, our, your, his, her,* and *their.*

My book
our house
your case
his complaint
her drill
their position.

Possessive pronouns used in positions other than before the thing possessed are *mine, ours, yours, his, hers,* and *theirs.*

The idea was mine.
He liked ours better than yours.
The decision was his.
The money was hers.
The thoughts were theirs.

2. Always make the plural of nouns ending in *-est* and *-ist* by adding *-s* to the singular form.

Singular	*Plural*
guest	guests
nest	nests
scientist	scientists
socialist	socialists

3. Make a distinction between *it's* and *its*. The contraction *it's* stands for "it is." The possessive pronoun *its* stands for "belonging to it."

He said, "It's almost impossible to guarantee safe travel."

This doctrine had lost its power by 1900.

4. Use the objective case of pronouns correctly. The nominative or subjective case of pronouns includes forms such as *I*, *we*, *he*, *she*, *who*, *they*, and *those*. The objective case includes forms such as *me*, *us*, *him*, *her*, *whom*, and *them*. The nominative case is used as the subject of a sentence or a clause.

I read Huizinga's books.

It was said that *he* was not the king's son.

Successive Russian leaders have believed that *they* were threatened by a strong Poland.

He spoke to *whoever* answered the telephone

The objective case should be used for the object of a preposition. Therefore you should say,

It was a matter between *him* and *me*.

Between you and me, I would say that the policy was wrong.

The objective case should be used as a direct object.

Bryan's campaign lifted *him* to sainthood among American farmers.

The objective case should be used as an indirect object.

The president gave *her* a cabinet position.

The objective case should be used as the subject or an objective of an infinitive. The infinitive is a verb form that includes the infinitive marker *to* and the dictionary form of the verb. Thus *to go, to be, to dwell,* and *to see* are all infinitives. The subject of the infinitive is a noun or pronoun before the infinitive that does the action the infinitive expresses.

King Leopold wanted *him* to go at once to Africa.

In this example the person designated by the objective pronoun *him* will go to Africa. Since he will do the going, the action expressed in the infinitive *to go,* the pronoun *him* is the subject of the infinitive and is in the objective case.

> The prime minister supposed both Russell and *me* to be damaged by the report.

In this example the pronoun before the infinitive receives the action of the infinitive—here an infinitive phrase. Do not use the objective case as a subject. Do not say, "Both Queen Elizabeth and *him* believed in going to war in the Netherlands." The idiomatic English way of expressing such a thought would be to say, "Both he and Queen Elizabeth believed in going to war in the Netherlands."

5. In *who* or *whom* clauses, the case of the pronoun is determined by how it is used in the clause, not how the clause is used in the sentence. (Many authorities now say that we should eliminate *whom* and use *who* for both the nominative and objective cases. Many others think the distinction should be preserved.)

Sometimes people eager to use *who* or *whom* correctly use *whom* where *who* is proper. The problem is especially acute in the use of the word *whomever,* a variant of *whom.* Some people will write things like this: "In the late nineteenth century, women and children worked for *whomever* would pay them pennies an hour for a fourteen-hour day." The fastidious writer of this sentence, knowing that the object of a preposition takes the objective case, writes the preposition *for* and puts *whomever* after it. But here the entire clause is the object of the preposition. The pronoun should be *whoever* because it is the subject of the clause. The pronoun in the clause is governed by how it is used in the clause, not by how the clause is used in the sentence. So the sentence should read, "In the late nineteenth century, women and children worked for *whoever* would pay them pennies an hour for a fourteen-hour day."

The same principle applies in a common sentence form where a parenthetical clause appears after the pronoun *who.* You should not write this:

> The Indians whom *Custer* thought were only a small band in fact numbered in the thousands.

You should write this instead:

The Indians who Custer thought were only a small band in fact numbered in the thousands.

The parenthetical clause *Custer thought* does not govern the clause *who were only a small band.* The subject of the verb *were* is the pronoun *who,* which must be in the subjective case.

6. Use commas in the following instances:

A. Commas set off independent clauses from each other. Independent clauses can nearly always stand by themselves as sentences.

The McNary-Haugen bill would have provided subsidies for American farmers, but President Coolidge vetoed it in 1927.

The Plains Indians loved ceremony, and Francis Parkman recorded some of their rites.

The people of the United States decided that they must give up Prohibition, for bootlegging and the gang wars that accompanied it were making cities run with blood.

B. Use commas to set off long introductory phrases and clauses.

Even after the transcontinental railroad was completed in 1867, some people still made the trip West by covered wagon.

After the American entry into the war in 1917, the victory of the Allied Powers over the Germans was assured.

C. Use commas to set off the items in a series.

President Franklin D. Roosevelt moved to solve problems of unemployment, banking, and extremism.

William Jennings Bryan campaigned for the presidency in 1896 by traveling 18,000 miles, making 600 speeches, and attacking the "monied interests."

D. Use commas to set off nonrestrictive clauses and phrases. Nonrestrictive clauses and phrases define other elements in a sentence. You can remove the nonrestrictive clause or phrase and still have an intelligible sentence.

Horatio Alger, who was a graduate of Harvard, wrote stories that appealed to the yearning of the poor to believe that they could become rich.

Henry David Thoreau, one of the greatest American writers, died of tuberculosis.

Do not use commas to set off restrictive clauses—clauses necessary if the main statement of the sentence is to be correctly understood.

The man *who robbed the bank on one day* came back the next and stole all the calendars.

E. Commas usually separate two or more adjectives used before a noun.

Ralph Waldo Emerson was a tall, frail, elegant man.

F. Use commas to set off parenthetical words and phrases.

Education was, to be sure, not merely a private matter.

Roosevelt, however, died before the Yalta agreements could be put to the test.

G. Place commas before quotation marks when a clause such as "he said" introduces the quotation.

Editor William Allen White said of his fellow Kansan Alf Landon, "I have never been able to visualize him as president."

H. Place commas within closing quotation marks.

"I have never been able to visualize him as president," editor William Allen White said of Alf Landon in 1935.

7. Make a distinction between restrictive and nonrestrictive clauses and phrases. Restrictive clauses and phrases are essential to the principal meaning of the sentence; nonrestrictive clauses and phrases are not. A nonrestrictive clause or phrase adds information that is interesting without being essential. Whether an element is restrictive or nonrestrictive depends on the author's purpose. Nonrestrictive clauses and phrases are set off by commas. Here are some examples.

Restrictive Clause:

The only candidate who could have beaten Thomas E. Dewey in 1948 was Harry Truman.

The clause *who could have beaten Thomas E. Dewey in 1948* is restrictive; it is necessary to the primary meaning of the sentence. If we wrote, "The only candidate was Harry Truman," we would have an entirely different meaning.

Nonrestrictive Clause:

Theodore Roosevelt, who happened to be facing an election campaign, made a strong pronouncement.

Here we have a clause that adds information not essential to the main statement of the sentence. We know who Theodore Roosevelt was. The main statement of the sentence can stand alone: *Theodore Roosevelt made a strong pronouncement.* The nonrestrictive clause *who happened to be facing an election campaign* adds interesting detail to the sentence, but because it is nonrestrictive, we set it off by commas.

Sometimes changing a clause or a phrase from restrictive to nonrestrictive changes the meaning.

In his novel, *Doomed by Grammar,* Weatherby treated sympathetically a corporate lawyer whose firm went bankrupt because of a dangling participle.

This sentence means that Weatherby wrote only one novel, and that it was entitled *Doomed by Grammar.* The commas indicate that the title provides additional but not essential information. If we leave out the commas, we have a slightly different meaning:

In his novel *Doomed by Grammar,* Weatherby treated sympathetically a corporate lawyer whose firm went bankrupt because of a dangling participle.

Here we have a comma setting off the introductory phrase from the rest of the sentence. We do not set off the title *Doomed by Grammar.* Thus the sentence could mean that Weatherby wrote several novels but that we are talking about only one of them, and so we must give its title.

8. Be sure that clauses acting as adjectives clearly modify the noun they are supposed to modify in the sentence. Modification is usually clearest when the modifying clause comes immediately after the noun it is modifying. Very often confusions in modification result when a writer tries to put too much in one sentence.

Don't say this:

> Bismarck's response to the German Socialist movement, which was his own way of assuring labor peace, effectively kept the Socialist party from obstructing his aims.

Was the German Socialist movement Bismarck's own way of assuring labor peace? No, though an uninformed reader might think so from this sentence. It would be better to make two clear sentences rather than one confusing one:

> Bismarck's response to the German Socialist movement effectively kept the Socialist party from obstructing his aims. He gained the loyalty of German workers by giving them a generous welfare program.

Sometimes the problem comes when writers follow the admirable policy of keeping the subject and the verb close together but then decide to tack an adjectival clause on at the end and so confuse an otherwise excellent sentence.

Don't say this:

> The Dreyfus Case weakened confidence in the French Army which unleashed furious passions in the French public.

The writer meant to say this:

> The Dreyfus Case, which unleashed furious passions in the French public, weakened confidence in the French Army.

9. Make your subject and your verb agree. Problems may arise when you have a prepositional phrase with a plural object after a singular subject.

Not this:

> His statement of grievances *were* read to the assembly.

But this:

> His statement of grievances *was* read to the assembly.

Use singular verbs after indefinite pronouns such as *anybody, everybody, anyone, everyone, somebody, someone, either, neither,* and *none.*

> Anybody in the group *is* likely to accept.

Everyone *was* ready.

Neither *was* possible.

None is occasionally used with a plural verb by some writers, though most writers still prefer to say, "None of the advantages *was* as great as the sum of the disadvantages."

Some collective words give problems. More traditional writers will say, "The majority of his followers was not convinced." But some writers will say, "The majority of his followers were not convinced," seeing "majority" as a collective noun that can take a plural verb. Here you must use your own judgment to decide which you will use.

10. Be sure that participial phrases opening a sentence modify the grammatical subject.

> Betrayed by his trust of unscrupulous friends, Warren G. Harding died just in time to receive a respectful funeral.

> Descending into Alsace, Louis XIV proclaimed it the "Garden of God."

You can make your prose incomprehensible and even ridiculous if you violate this rule.

> Rocketing toward the moon, Americans stayed up late by their television sets to see the photographs sent back by our astronauts.

This sentence means that Americans rocketed towards the moon and sat up late by their television sets. But the writer meant to say that while the astronauts were rocketing toward the moon, Americans at home stayed up to watch television.

Avoid making an opening participle modify an expletive *it*. (The expletive *it* is the pronoun without a referent and used as a subject. We say, "It will rain," without having the pronoun refer to another noun. We say, "It is hard to see what he wanted," using the pronoun as the grammatical subject.) Avoid constructions like this: "Steaming toward Europe, it seemed wise to him to hide from photographers on the ship." It is better to say, "Steaming towards Europe, he tried to avoid photographers on the ship."

11. When you use adverbs such as *only, even, hardly, nearly, almost,* and *just* to modify adjectives, place them just before the adjective. Don't say, "Edward VIII only ruled a few months."

Say, "Edward VIII ruled only a few months." Don't say, "Germany did not even gain an acknowledgment that Austria-Hungary might also have had some responsibility for beginning World War I." Say, "Germany did not gain even an acknowledgment that Austria-Hungary might also have had some responsibility for starting World War I."

12. Use "hardly"as a negative in itself. Do not use it with another negative. Don't say, "Adams was not hardly ready to face the real implications of democratic government"; say, "Adams was hardly ready to face the implications of democratic government."

13. Do not break the parallel form of a series. English and American writers often use words or phrases in series, often in units of three. We speak of exorcising a demon in the Middle Ages "by bell, book, and candle." We write sentences like this: "The moral principle of seeking the greatest good for the greatest number motivated Rousseau, Bentham, and Mill." The units in the series must stand as grammatical equals. Therefore you should not write sentences like this: "Richelieu wanted three things for France—authority for the king, an end to religious strife, and he also wanted secure 'natural' frontiers." The first two elements of this faulty series are nouns modified by prepositional phrases, but the last element is a clause. The sentence should be rewrittern like this: "Richelieu wanted three things for France—authority for the king, an end to religious strife, and secure 'natural' frontiers."

14. Use a colon only after a complete clause. Use the colon to introduce a statement that elaborates on the thought of the previous clause. That elaboration may be a quotation (often a block quotation), or a list, or simply another clause. The colon before the block quotation has been frequently illustrated in this book. Here is a sentence that uses the colon to introduce a list that elaborates the thought of the clause.

> Franklin Roosevelt faced a multitude of problems: catastrophic unemployment, daily failures of banks, and a demoralized American people.

Some writers substitute a dash for the colon:

> Franklin Roosevelt faced a multitude of problems—catastrophic unemployment, daily failures of banks, and a demoralized American people.

The dash is more emphatic.

The colon may be followed by a clause elaborating the statement made in the first clause.

> President Harry S. Truman made one of the greatest advances in the fight for civil rights for American blacks: He desegregated the armed forces.

15. Do not join independent clauses with commas alone. Do not write this:

> The Fugitive Slave Act required free states to return escaped slaves to their owners in the South, in effect it removed the limits of safety for fleeing slaves from the Ohio River to the Canadian border.

You can use a semicolon to make such a division:

> The Fugitive Slave Act required free states to return escaped slaves to thier owners in the South; in effect it removed the limits of safety for fleeing slaves from the Ohio River to the Canadian border.

16. Observe the difference between *lie* and *lay*. To *lie* means to recline; *to lay* means to put something down so that it reclines. We lie down to go to sleep; we lay our watches on the table beside the bed.

Most of the problems arise from the past forms of these verbs, for the simple past tense of *lie* is *lay:* "The chief responsibility for the Confederate defeat at Gettysburg lay on the shoulders of Robert E. Lee." The past tense of *lay* is *laid:* "Many Southerners, unwilling to acknowledge a flaw in their hero Lee, laid the blame for the defeat at Gettysburg on Longstreet."

The past participle of *lie* is *lain,* and the past participle of *lay* is *laid:*

> The myth of Lee's invincibility has lain in the heart of the South for over a century.

But modern students of the battle have laid the myth to rest.

17. Never use the apostrophe to form a plural. Do not say 1960's or "The Wilsons' were happy together." The apostrophe is used to form the possessive case in ways stated above; it is not used to make words plural.

18. Avoid vulgarisms such as "alot"and "alright." These are efforts to combine two words and make them one. You should speak about "a lot" of people and of Joseph McCarthy's view that it was "all right" if innocent people suffered by his public attacks.

19. Avoid confusion in making pronouns refer to antecedents. Pronouns stand for nouns. Definite pronouns such as *he, she, it, him, her, they, them* and *their* stand for nouns that usually appear somewhere before them in a sentence or paragraph. Be sure to make the pronoun reference clear, even if you have to revise the sentence considerably. Don't do this:

> The Czechs disdained the Slovaks because they were more cosmopolitan.

To whom does the pronoun *they* refer? Were the Czechs or the Slovaks more cosmopolitan? You must rewrite the sentence:

> The more cosmopolitan Czechs disdained the more rural Slovaks.

20. Maintain parallel forms. The coordinate conjunctions *and, but, or, nor,* and *for* must join grammatically equal parts of a sentence. You disrupt parallel forms when you join grammatically unequal parts of a sentence.

> Churchill told the English people that he had nothing to offer them but *"blood, toil, tears,* and *sweat."*

BOOK REVIEWS

Reviewing books is an essential part of the historian's profession. Your teacher may tell you to write a book review of a book pertaining to the course you are taking. Before you write a review, look at journals that carry reviews of books written about the region and the period you are studying in the course. *The American Historical Review* reviews books about all the regions of the world and all periods. But *The Journal of Modern History* carries reviews only of books written about the period after 1500.

An hour or two spent in the periodical room of your library reading book reviews will help you understand the form and imitate it in your own review. If you find several scholarly reviews of the book you are reviewing yourself, you may learn a great deal about the book and its author, and you will also see some issues that you might choose to write about. Here are some pointers that will also help:

1. Always give the author's major theme, his or her motive for writing the book. You will most often find that motive expressed in the preface, which you should always read.
2. Summarize the evidence the author presents.
3. Identify the author, but do not waste time on needless or extravagant claims about him or her. It is a cliché to say that the author is "well-qualified" to write about a book.
4. Avoid lengthy comments on the style of the book. It's fine to say that the style is good or bad, interesting or tedious. If a book is especially well written or incomprehensible, you may quote a sentence to illustrate a good or bad style, but don't belabor the point.
5. Avoid generalizations such as, "This book is very interesting," or "This book is very boring." If you do your job in the review, readers should be able to see whether the book is boring or interesting without your having to tell them so.
6. Avoid passionate attacks on the book. It is always a mistake to launch an emotional attack on a book merely because you do not like it. Scholarship is not always courteous, but it should be. Reviewers who launch savage attacks on books usually make fools of themselves. They may even win friends for the book they are seeking to demolish.
7. Do not feel *compelled* to say negative things about the book. Sometimes reviewers feel that they have not done their job unless they have something bad to say about the book. If you find important inaccuracies, say so. If you disagree with the writer's interpretations here and there, say that, too. But do not feel that you are obliged to say something bad about the book even if you find nothing obvious to criticize. Petty complaints about the book may make you look foolish or unfair. Don't waste your time by pointing out typographical errors unless you think they change the meaning of the text.
8. Judge the book the author has written. You may wish the author had written a different book. You might choose to write a different

book. But the author has written *this* book. If the book did not need to be written; if it adds nothing to our knowledge of the field; if it makes conclusions unwarranted by the evidence, say so. But don't review the book as if it should be another book.

9. Always remember that every good book has flaws. The author may make some minor errors in fact or some questionable judgments. Even so, the book may be extremely valuable. Don't condemn a book outright because you find some mistakes. Try to judge the book as a whole.

10. Try to bring something from your own experience—your reading, your thoughts, your recollections—to the book review. You should know more about the subject than the book tells you. Try to use that independent knowledge to explain the book and your attitudes toward it. Try to make use of a broad part of your education when you write a review. If you know other books or if you have thoughts about some facts the author may have overlooked, mention them in your review.

11. Avoid writing as if you possess independent knowledge of the author's subject when in fact you have taken all you know from the book itself. Don't pretend to be an expert when you are not.

12. Quote selectively from the book you are reviewing. Quotations give some of the tone of the original, and they may express thoughts in a sharp and pungent way. The prose of the author whose work you are reviewing may help spice up your own review.

13. Avoid long chunks of quotation. You must show your readers that you have absorbed the book you are reviewing. If you give them too many long quotations, they may think that you are asking them to do the reflection and analysis you should have done yourself.

Appendix

Essay Examinations

Essay examinations are not like the other kinds of papers that I have discussed in this book. Nevertheless, as the name "essay exam" insists, they are essays—essays to be done within a given time in circumstances where you must rely entirely on your memory, without the aid of notes or the reference room of a library. Essay examinations test what you know and how you think about what you know. They are to some degree artificial creations; historians do not write under the strictures of the standard essay exam format. They write and revise, go back to their sources, and revise some more.

Such exams are, however, perhaps the most comprehensive test of how much you have learned in an academic course, and they are so much a part of the Western academic scene that you doubtless already have much experience with them. The best examinations allow you to show your knowledge about the facts and some sources for those facts and to prove that you can make some judgments about the material. Here are some sample questions that you may find on an examination in the history of the Protestant Reformation:

Trace the career of Martin Luther from the Indulgence Controversy in 1517 to his appearance before the Diet of Worms in 1521.

This question asks you for narrative. You must tell Luther's story from one important moment in his life to another. The question does not ask for an explicit argument. It assumes that you have read about Luther in your textbooks or in several other assigned readings, that you have followed his career in the lectures, that you have given his life some thought, and that you can repeat the major events relating to him in these years. You are not being asked for a list of happenings. You are being asked to write an essay, to tell a story, to construct a narrative. An essay examination requires an essay! Although we might suppose that such a statement might be self-evident, many students defeat themselves in examinations and get lower grades than they should when they try to do something other than write an essay. They write a series of short answers without any effort to tie those short answers into a coherent story, and they do not fulfill the assignment.

The question about Luther assumes that important changes took place between 1517 and 1521. You should sketch those changes in your answer. What was Luther in 1517? He was an obscure monk in a remote part of Germany who attacked the sale of indulgences supposed to release souls from Purgatory. What was he in 1521? He was known all over Europe as a rebel against Church authority, excommunicated by the pope, and called to defend himself before the Emperor of the Holy Roman Empire.

The differences in Luther between the first date and the last define your answer. What happened? Why? In an examination question calling for a narrative, try to answer both questions. Knowing what happened tells your teacher that you have learned the material; giving your argument about why it happened tells the teacher that you have thought about what you know. Take a moment to jot down a few words to outline your answer. For this question you might write down the following. (These particular words may not make any sense to you if you do not know something about Luther. That is all right. I use them only to show a method.)

```
95 theses disputation at Heidelberg

Meeting with Cajetan

Justification by faith

Leipzig disputation with Eck

Babylonian captivity

Other writings of 1520

Papal excommunication

Appearance before the Emperor in April
```

You can expand each of these headings to a paragraph. The headings happen to refer to events in chronological order, each important to Luther's career. Any teacher would be pleased to have you recount them as the answer to the question phrased above. By pausing to write them in a brief outline (which could be even more brief than this version), you can work off the anxiety we all have at the start of an examination, you organize your thoughts, and you start thinking before you write. You will not then be writing blindly as the exam goes along. This scratch outline resembles the finger exercises musicians do before a concert or the limbering up of athletes before a game. A brief outline helps you include everything you should include and provides shape to your thoughts.

You may recognize uncertainties about the events of these years. Even on an examination you should comment on gaps in our knowledge. Let your reader know that you recognize puzzles in the evidence. Scholars have argued vehemently over the date of Luther's "discovery" of his major doctrine, justification by faith. You can't solve the problem in an exam; you can show that you know it exists. Teachers are impressed by such things. Neither in your essay exams or your other writing should you try to grind off the rough edges of historical study. History does not hold together smoothly. Don't pretend it does. If your teacher is trying to get you to demonstrate some of your own thinking during an examination, you may get a question like this:

> Compare Luther's view of God and the church with that of Thomas More.

Comparison questions are popular in history courses. They force students to think about similarities and differences. (Your teacher may write, "Compare and contrast Luther's view with that of Thomas More." But any comparison requires us to declare not only the similarities but also the differences between two or more items.)

Be sure to pick out the *significant* areas of comparison. Some comparisons are significant for this question. We know, for example, that More and Luther liked eggs but that while Luther usually drank beer, More usually drank wine. These items, while interesting, have nothing to do with the question. If you have studied hard for an examination, you may be tempted to pour all your knowledge into the question. Avoid that temptation. Answer the question as it has been asked. A hard-pressed teacher will not have time in grading your paper to give you the benefit of the doubt. If you give no clear answer to the question, your teacher will assume that you do not know the answer, and you will not get any special credit for the flood of confused knowledge that you pour out on your paper. Answer the question. Limit what you say to the job the question asks you to do.

Start your comparison with a brief outline:

Both More and Luther wanted reform in the Church.

Both of them believed that God was all-powerful and mysterious.

Both believed that human beings had no worth in themselves except as God gave them worth.

Both of them feared the judgment of God, but Luther feared death and More feared hell.

Both demanded an infallible authority. Luther's authority was the Word of God as revealed in the Bible; More's authority was the tradition of the Catholic Church.

Luther wanted reform in doctrine; reform in morals was secondary to him. More wanted reform in morals; he thought that if doctrines had been deemed essential to salvation by the church, they could not be changed.

Luther wanted to cease the veneration of the saints and to rid worship of saints' relics; More wanted to keep both.

Both believed religion was necessary if society were to endure.

In the examination situation when you may have only a half hour or perhaps an hour to write on such a question, you would probably abbreviate your outline considerably. You could, for example, write for the above question,

reform God hell authority Word of God/Church reform in doctrine/reform in morals saints and relics religion/society

You could list many more items for comparison between Luther and More. Your quick jottings here can start you off on writing a good essay. It seems to be more natural in comparisons to begin with the similarities and then to pass to the differences. I have suggested here a means of concluding the essay with a sort of flourish, ending it on an important matter about which the two men agreed.

Exams requiring arguments are both difficult and challenging. They may take several forms. Some teachers like to ask *what if* questions. Such questions require you to demonstrate your knowledge of what did happen and the connections that you perceive between various people and events. For example, a teacher might ask you to speculate on what might have happened had the British won the American War for Independence. You might then argue that Napoleon would never have sold the Louisiana Territories to the British, though he was willing in 1804 to sell them to the weak and distant independent United States. Other consequences would have followed. A question like this allows you to play in a serious way with some of the data and to see more clearly some relations that might otherwise have been obscure. Then, using your knowledge, you must argue your own point of view.

The point of an argument on an examination is not to prove one side or another beyond any doubt. I hope you know by now that historians seldom prove anything beyond any doubt. You cannot resolve all doubts and eliminate all contrary opinions in the few minutes you have on an examination. You can, however, show that you know the material and that you can think about it intelligently. You will always impress your teacher if you can rapidly survey the arguments opposite to your point of view and show how you disagree with them. Many kinds of arguments may come up in exams or in history papers.

Your teacher may ask you to compare the opinions of two historians on a controversial matter and argue for the correctness of one of them. You may have to argue who was more guilty for the beginning of World War I, the Germans or the Russians. You may be required to argue whether Reconstruction following the Civil War was a success or a failure, or whether economics or political influences contributed more to the emancipation of women. The subjects are endless. It is worth repeating that the aim of such questions is not to have you resolve the issues but to demonstrate that you know the material and that you can think about it. Asking you to make an argument is a good way of preventing you from merely repeating the information you have taken from your reading and the lectures.

Often teachers will ask you why something happened. "Why did France put up such a stiff fight against the Germans in 1914 only to collapse in a little over a month in 1940?" Your teacher will expect a carefully reasoned discussion of the various possibilities that may be suggested by this question. You will have to consider the differences between 1914 and 1940, the argument that the French people lost their enthusiasm for their own government between the wars, and the counterargument that the Germans simply employed tactics that would have defeated any country that tried to use the tactics of the French army in 1940. A *why* question always demands a discussion. It nearly always implies that there are several different points of view and that you should demonstrate some acquaintance with those various views and then arrive at your own conclusion.

To show that you do know the material, you must be specific. You should be able to mention books and authors and to give their points of view. You should by all means be able to give specific examples to illustrate your generalizations. Do not say, "Some people claimed they came on the Reformation consciousness without being influenced by Luther." Say, "Ulrich Zwingli in Zurich claimed he came to the Reformation without reading Luther; if he did, we have a further argument for the belief that the Protestant Reformation would have come even if Luther had never been born." Specific information carries authority; vague generalizations do not.

Much of your success in examinations will depend on how well you prepare. Always read with a notebook at hand. Jot down the main points of authors, points you can usually learn quickly by reading the introductions to books and the first and last paragraphs of articles. Write down names and next to them write their significance. Write down major events and use a few words to explain why they are important.

A good preparation for an examination is to make up questions of your own on the material. You will discover that you can be extremely successful in guessing what the questions may be if you have paid close attention to the emphases of the teacher in lectures and discussions. Teachers come to questions in the same way you can: They ask themselves what they can ask you to make sure you have done the assigned work and have paid attention in class. Only rarely do teachers give questions on matters they have not covered in class. If you listen attentively and concentrate your reading on those things most important to the teacher, you will almost certainly be able to guess the general shape of the questions to come on the examination. If you write out your guesses, you will shape the information before you go to the exam. You will be pleasantly surprised at your ability to guess what you will see on the exam.

If you have time to write out some sketches of answers to those questions, so much the better. You will learn the extent of your knowledge. If you do not know things, you will learn your weaknesses and the gaps in your knowledge, and you can set yourself to learning. You will imprint what you do on your mind, and when the real exam comes, you will discover that this information will be there in your memory where you can retrieve it without the nervous strain that sometimes comes in exams.

One other tip: When you have an exam coming up in a history course, go to the reference room in your library and look up articles in encyclopedias and in other reference works about the people and the events likely to be on the test. Your teacher has provided information in lectures and discussion, and you have done the reading in the course. All this imprints information in your mind. But very often you will be helped to remember this information if you find it in another form—an encyclopedia article, for example—and read it there. The more different ways you can study the same information, the more thoroughly you will be able to recall that information and use it effectively on examinations.

Credits

Index